Edna St. Vincent Millay

Revised Edition

Twayne's United States Authors Series

Kenneth Eble, Editor
University of Utah

TUSAS 116

EDNA ST. VINCENT MILLAY
(1892–1950)
Photograph courtesy of Vassar College Library.

Edna St. Vincent Millay

Revised Edition

By Norman A. Brittin

Auburn University

Twayne Publishers • *Boston*

Edna St. Vincent Millay, Revised Edition

Norman A. Brittin

Copyright © 1982 by G.K. Hall & Company
All Rights Reserved
Published by Twayne Publishers
A Division of G. K. Hall & Company
70 Lincoln Street
Boston, Massachusetts 02111

Book Production by Marne B. Sultz

Book Design by Barbara Anderson

Printed on permanent/durable acid-free
paper and bound in the United States of
America.

**Library of Congress Cataloging in
Publication Data**

Brittin, Norman A.
Edna St. Vincent Millay.

(Twayne's United States authors series;
TUSAS 116)
Bibliography: p. 153
Includes index.
1. Millay, Edna St. Vincent,
1892–1950—
Criticism and interpretation.
I. Title.   II. Title: Edna Saint Vincent
Millay.   III. Series.
PS3525.I495Z62 1982 811'.52 82-12049
ISBN 0-8057-7362-2

To Ruth
Always Involved
Always Invaluable

Contents

About the Author

Norman A. Brittin, Hollifield Professor Emeritus of English Literature at Auburn University, received the Ph.D. from the University of
Washington. In his long teaching career he has been on the faculties of
the Universities of Southern California, Utah, Washington, Chicago,
Puerto Rico, and La Laguna in the Canary Islands, where he was
Fulbright Lecturer in American Literature. He was also the recipient of
a Ford Fellowship at Columbia and Harvard, cowinner of the Warshaw
Award for the Humanities (*Western Humanities Review*), and a Fellow at
the Folger Shakespeare Library. For ten years he served as coeditor of the
Southern Humanities Review. Dr. Brittin's own poetry has been published
in many magazines and reviews, and he took part during the 1940s in
forming a new poetry magazine, *Experiment,* of which he was Acting
Editor in 1944. His critical and scholarly work has appeared in the
*Western Humanities Review, Sewanee Review, Antioch Review, Shakespeare
Quarterly, PMLA, Ball State University Forum,* and *Southern Humanities
Review,* and he is the author of *Thomas Middleton* in the Twayne English
Authors Series.

Preface to the Revised Edition

This revision differs in several respects from the first edition. Emphasizing only those experiences in Millay's life that were of primary importance for poetry, and generally treating them in less detail, I have reduced the space given to her biography. By doing so, I have been able to discuss her prose writings, to augment and particularize the discussion of Millay as a feminist, and to include consideration of Millay's poetry in relation to the poetic movement now known as "High Modernism." In addition, I have discussed some poems which received less attention in the first edition, and I have, of course, updated the bibliography.

Since 1966 there have been a few advances in Millay scholarship. Publication of the bibliographies of John J. Patton and of Judith Nierman has supplied excellent tools for research. When the new Millay biography by Nancy Milford appears, it ought to provide answers to many questions, for the author has enjoyed access to more material than any other biographer. But a Millay concordance and a study of Millay's prosody are still much needed.

In this book, following the Chronology and Chapter 1, which is biographical, Millay's works are treated in a prevailingly chronological order. Chapter 2 is on her early poetry through *The Harp-Weaver and Other Poems*, Chapter 3 on her prose, and Chapter 4 on her dramatic works. In Chapter 5 the remainder of her poetry is discussed. Chapter 6 is concerned with Millay and feminism, and Chapter 7 supplies an account of the critical reception of Millay's work and an estimate of her achievement.

For help I received in revising this book my grateful thanks are due to Norma Millay, Alice Baur Hodges, John J. Patton, Walter S. Minot, and my colleague Patrick Morrow.

Norman A. Brittin

Auburn University

Introduction

Some poets lead retired and uneventful lives; others not only devote themselves to the composition of verse but take part in worldly activities of business, war, travel, politics, and councils of men. Such poets as Chaucer, Lord Byron, Matthew Arnold, William Morris, and Archibald MacLeish led active lives. So did Edna St. Vincent Millay; as early as 1924 Harriet Monroe commented on the crowded activity of the poet's youth. After her marriage, although Millay settled at Steepletop, in Austerlitz, New York, she traveled, lived in New York and Paris, gave readings all over the country, took part in the Sacco-Vanzetti protest, and responded vigorously to the impact of World War II. She became known not only as a "popular poet" but as a "public poet."

Millay's manifold activities are doubtless related to her versatility. A woman with talents that afforded many possibilities for a career, she had musical training and might have been a pianist or a song-writer; she also had theatrical experience and might have become an actress. She could have succeeded in prose and did, in fact, publish short stories and satires.

Arthur DuBois analyzed Millay in terms of the precocious child, the poet, the woman, and the mystic. For each of these terms there is in Millay a corresponding and contrasting quality. For the child—suggesting innocence, wonder, and the need for special consideration—there is the tomboy and tease. Full of swagger and banter, she is a kind of Tom Sawyer who wants to do things in a "highfalutin" style. For the poet, full of lyrical feeling and sensitivity, there is the satirist. Ready with the wisecrack, she is the author of the Nancy Boyd sketches, and in her letters she frequently snaps a satirical lash and is indignant and ironic. For the woman, there is the feminist demanding her rights. She insists on being regarded not merely as dependent woman but on playing an independent role in love and impressing men as capable of being detached and analytical—as having a "man's attitude." And for the mystic, there is the agnostic, the self-conscious modern, who is much aware of being cut off from traditional religion and standing alone in the midst of the indifferent universe that Hardy and Housman presented.

Thus, one might interpret Millay as a person who combined a teasing boy, an indignant satirist, a schoolmarmish feminist, and a tough-minded agnostic. Yet she is also all the things DuBois mentioned. From these paradoxes, one supposes, come Millay's variety and her elusiveness stressed by Miriam Gurko, the attitude of gallantry-in-the-midst-of-tears, and the frequent irony in her writing. Hers is a classic case of the romantic irony found in Heinrich Heine and in other romantic poets. She has been compared to Byron; certainly, like him, she was an unusual combination of heart and head; she was romantic at heart but had respect for classic poetry and a strong tendency toward satire.

Millay earned a reputation as one of the leading poets of her time. Being a woman, she wrote with a great sensitivity about personal relationships and about the condition of the world. Her attitudes, especially those regarding love and the situation of women, exemplified those of the twentieth century; but she was more than a woman poet. She was a modern humanist and a radical; her humanism and her radicalism were immutable qualities. She was typical of the World War I generation that gave the 1920s their characteristic tone, but much of her writing transcends the 1920s.

Her reputation suffered because of her propaganda poems of World War II, and with changing fashions she was, for a generation or more, cast into a limbo of critical neglect. Renewed interest in her work is growing, however, in large part because of the renewed interest in feminism.

N. A. B.

Acknowledgments

For the use of certain materials, I am grateful to the following:

Norma Millay for permission to quote from the following sources published by Harper and Brothers: *Collected Poems,* copyright 1917, 1921, 1922, 1923, 1928, 1931, 1933, 1934, 1936, 1937, 1938, 1939, 1940, 1941, 1950 by Edna St. Vincent Millay; copyright 1945, 1946, 1951, 1952, 1953, 1954, 1956 by Norma Millay Ellis. *Three Plays,* copyright 1926 by Edna St. Vincent Millay; copyright 1953 by Norma Millay Ellis. *The King's Henchman,* copyright 1927 by Edna St. Vincent Millay; copyright 1954 by Norma Millay Ellis. *The Princess Marries the Page,* copyright 1932 by Edna St. Vincent Millay; copyright 1960 by Norma Millay Ellis. *Flowers of Evil,* copyright 1936 by George Dillon and Edna St. Vincent Millay; copyright 1963 by Norma Millay Ellis and George Dillon. *Conversation at Midnight,* copyright 1937 by Edna St. Vincent Millay; copyright 1964 by Norma Millay Ellis. *Huntsman, What Quarry?,* copyright 1939 by Edna St. Vincent Millay. *Make Bright the Arrows,* copyright 1940 by Edna St. Vincent Millay. *The Murder of Lidice,* copyright 1942 by Edna St. Vincent Millay. *Distressing Dialogues,* copyright 1924 by Edna St. Vincent Millay; copyright 1951 by Norma Millay Ellis. *Letters of Edna St. Vincent Millay,* copyright 1952 by Norma Millay Ellis.

Mrs. Arthur Davison Ficke for permission to consult material in the Arthur Davison Ficke Collection in the Yale University Library.

The Yale University Library for permission to publish information from the Arthur Davison Ficke Collection and other material by and about Edna St. Vincent Millay.

The editors of *Ball State University Forum* for permission substantially to reprint my article "Edna St. Vincent Millay's 'Nancy Boyd' Stories," copyright 1969 by *Ball State University Forum.*

Chronology

1892 Edna St. Vincent Millay born 22 February at Rockland, Maine; first child of Henry Tolman Millay and Cora Buzzelle Millay, who encouraged her daughter to excel in music and poetry.

1900 Parents divorced.

1905–1909 Attended high school in Camden, Maine; became editor-in-chief of school magazine.

1906–1910 Poems published by *St. Nicholas Magazine.*

1912 Attracted attention of Caroline B. Dow, who enabled her to enroll in college. Attracted national attention for "Renascence" upon publication of *The Lyric Year* in November.

1913 Attended Barnard College to prepare for entrance to Vassar College, which she entered in autumn.

1915–1917 Played in Vassar productions of several plays; wrote and took the leading part in *The Princess Marries the Page;* graduated with A.B., 1917.

1917 *Renascence and Other Poems.* To New York in the fall; acted with Provincetown Players.

1918 Lived in poverty in Greenwich Village while acting. Love affairs with Floyd Dell, Arthur Davison Ficke, and others.

1919 Poems (and stories under pseudonym Nancy Boyd) in *Ainslee's.* Finished *Aria da Capo* and directed it for Provincetown Players; first performance, 5 December.

1920 Publications in *Vanity Fair* and *Reedy's Mirror.* Received $100 prize from *Poetry* for "The Bean-Stalk." *A Few Figs from Thistles* and *Aria da Capo.* Left for Europe to write for *Vanity Fair.*

1921   European travel. *Two Slatterns and a King, The Lamp and the Bell,* and *Second April.*

1922   With $500 advance on *Hardigut,* a novel, brought her mother to Europe. Health poor.

1923   February, returned to the United States. Received Pulitzer Prize for poetry. Serious illness. Married Eugen Jan Boissevain, 18 July. *The Harp-Weaver and Other Poems.*

1924   January, began reading tours. With husband, toured Orient. *Distressing Dialogues* (by Nancy Boyd).

1925   Reading tours. On 15 June, Honorary Litt.D. degree from Tufts College. She and husband bought farm (Steepletop) at Austerlitz, New York; their home for the rest of their lives.

1927   Metropolitan Opera premiere of *The King's Henchman,* 17 February. August, participated in Boston protests against execution of Sacco and Vanzetti.

1928   *The Buck in the Snow.* Ten sonnets of "Epitaph for the Race of Man" in St. Louis *Post-Dispatch* (December).

1929   Elected to National Institute of Arts and Letters; *Poems Selected for Young People.*

1931   *Fatal Interview.* Received Helen Haire Levinson Prize for sonnets in *Poetry* (October, 1930).

1932   *The Princess Marries the Page.* On 25 December, first of a series of eight national radio broadcasts on which she very successfully read her poems.

1933   Presented Prix Femina to Willa Cather, 2 February. Laureate of General Federation of Women's Clubs, 22 May. Litt.D. degrees from University of Wisconsin and Russell Sage College.

1934   *Wine from These Grapes,* 1 November.

1935   Summer, worked with George Dillon on Baudelaire translation.

1936   April, *Flowers of Evil* (with George Dillon). Manuscript of *Conversation at Midnight* destroyed 2 May in hotel fire, Sanibel Island, Florida. Summer, injury to nerves of back. December-May 1937, in New York rewriting *Conversation at Midnight.*

1937   June, honorary L.H.D. from New York University, honorary Litt.D. from Colby College. *Conversation at Midnight.*

1939   Intense interest in international situation. *Huntsman, What Quarry?*

1940   May, began writing propaganda. November, elected to American Academy of Arts and Letters. *Make Bright the Arrows.*

1941   Recorded her poems for RCA Victor. *Collected Sonnets.*

1942   *The Murder of Lidice.*

1943   Received Gold Medal of the Poetry Society of America, 31 January.

1944   Summer, nervous breakdown; unable to write for two years.

1949   Eugen Jan Boissevain died 30 August in Boston of a stroke after an operation. After hospitalization, she returned to live alone at Steepletop.

1950   While living alone in great grief, continued writing until her death of heart failure on 19 October.

1952   *Letters of Edna St. Vincent Millay.*

1954   *Mine the Harvest.*

1956   *Collected Poems.*

1973   November, the Millay Colony for the Arts founded at Steepletop.

1980   The Edna St. Vincent Millay Society *Newsletter.*

1981   Edna St. Vincent Millay Stamp issued, 10 July.

Chapter One

"These Were the Things That Bounded Me"

Carrying a pail of blueberries she had just picked in the pastures outside Camden, Maine, Edna St. Vincent Millay, a tiny red-headed girl of twenty, approached her home in the town and saw her mother waiting on the doorstep with a letter in her hand. The letter, addressed to "E. Vincent Millay, Esq.," was from Ferdinand Earle, sponsor of *The Lyric Year*. It expressed his enthusiasm over a poem entitled "Renaissance" and—prematurely—his confidence that the poem would be awarded the $500 first prize in the *Lyric Year* contest. This vivid little episode brought together at that moment of 1912 three of the essential elements of Edna St. Vincent Millay's poetic career. These were the precocious talent of the young woman; the Maine background of pasture, mountain, and seashore; and the strong and inspiring figure of the poet's mother, Cora Millay.

"Tall Elms, My Roots Go Down"

Mrs. Millay was a woman of musical talent who had been a singer—a woman independent enough to divorce her husband, the charming—perhaps brilliant, but undependable—poker-playing Henry Tolman Millay, a school principal and superintendent. Tough enough to earn a living for herself and her three daughters as a practical nurse, Mrs. Millay was so zealous for her children's development that, even though they lacked creature comforts at times, she saw that they had books, music lessons, and incentive to express themselves and to excel. The four Millays were a close, female family group. Though the girls lacked the presence of a father to take as a model—which so many women of achievement have had during girlhood—they were quick-minded, imaginative, and responsive to the opportunities provided by their mother (with an occasional gift from the father) in a small resort and mill town.

New England respect for education and New England self-reliance and composure in the face of poverty were important parts of the home environment in which Vincent—apparently she was never called Edna by the family—was reared. Furthermore, in the Millay home it was more important to read, write, sing, learn, and be creative than to slave at dusting, mopping, mending, and cooking. Mrs. Millay taught Vincent the elements of music, and for three years the girl studied to become a concert pianist with John Tufts, a retired music teacher; but about 1908 he decided that her hands were too tiny to allow her to have such a career.[1] She had acquired, however, a considerable amount of musical knowledge and skill, which were to aid her later.

At thirteen Vincent was "The Newest Freshman" in the Camden High School. In a composition with that title published in the school magazine, she mentioned her excitement while reading a criticism of Darwin's theory.[2] Probably few Maine girls of thirteen were stimulated by such reading. Norma Millay, Vincent's younger sister, attributes this interest in scientific matters to their mother's constant encouragement to read books and magazines.

Vincent was also writing verse, and in 1905 she joined the St. Nicholas League (for aspiring writers under eighteen) of *St. Nicholas Magazine,* which accepted "Forest Trees," her first poem to be published (October 1906). The third stanza of the poem reveals an awareness of geologic processes and an imaginative concept of the vast reaches of time through which the forest persists:

> Around you all is change—where now is land
> Swift vessels plowed to foam the seething main;
> Kingdoms have risen, and the fire fiend's hand
> Has crushed them to their mother earth again;
> And through it all ye stand, and still will stand
> Till ages yet to come have owned your reign.

Reminiscent of Tennyson's *In Memoriam* (Section 123): "There rolls the deep where grew the tree," it is also prophetic of "Epitaph for the Race of Man."

"The Land of Romance," one of five other poems accepted by *St. Nicholas,* received the Gold Badge of the St. Nicholas League and was reprinted in *Current Literature* (April 1907) along with E. A. Robinson's "Miniver Cheevy" and work by Thomas Bailey Aldrich, Edwin Markham, and Witter Bynner. It was thought a remarkable production for a fourteen-year-old; with its trite, romantic tags it shows influence of Poe and decadent poets of the 1890s. In general, Millay's juvenilia are romantic—rather Tennysonian—and show her interest in trying out various meters.

In high school Vincent had parts in class plays and afterwards did some acting in amateur theatricals and with stock companies traveling through.[3] During the summer of 1907 she worked as a typist; in her leisure she wrote her first sonnet, "Old Letters."[4] After graduation she took occasional jobs, usually as a stenographer for summer visitors;[5] and she engaged in usual girls' activities of a small seaside town. While her mother was away working in the summer of 1911, she did most of the cooking at home while also writing poems.

She submitted poems to many editors, but none was published. Only her family and a few other townspeople were aware of her writing. One would imagine that Vincent felt uncertainty and frustration during this period. At least she had the advantage—as did Wordsworth—of a daily life "incorporated with the beautiful and permanent forms of nature."[6] Gorham Munson compares the Penobscot country to the English Lake District and calls it "ideal Poet's country."[7] Views of mountains, woods, fields, sea, and coastline became indelibly impressed upon an adolescent heart. The waves, the winds whirling spray over rocks and wharves, seaweed and green piles, gulls tacking into the breeze—there was no item of this coastal life that she did not remember. She could never free herself of the hold which nature in this particular place had upon her; and she never wished to. When she was past forty, she wrote of the Penobscot area as her *pays,* like that part of the world a Frenchman really loves, "bounded only by the horizon of his early associations. . . ."[8]

"The First . . . to Think My Poetry of Some Consequence"

When news came in late February 1912 that her father was seriously ill, Vincent, barely twenty, traveled to Kingman, Maine, a village a hundred miles north where Henry Millay was living. While he recovered, she stayed a week at the home of his physician, where she received an important announcement. Mrs. Millay had read of a contest for a proposed annual anthology, *The Lyric Year,* and she suggested that her daughter come home and submit something. Vincent completed "Renaissance" and sent it in, along with a dramatic soliloquy in verse entitled "Interim."

Slogging through the 10,000 entries received ("piles of disgustingly awful *rot* . . ."),[9] Ferdinand Earle rejoiced when he read "Renaissance," though the simplicity of its opening lines caused it almost to be discarded by a friend helping to sift manuscripts. Not taking into account the other two judges, Earle rushed off the overhasty announcement of success which must have kindled in Vincent and the other Millays tingling satisfaction and joy.

During correspondence between Vincent and Earle she accepted his proposal to change her title to "Renascence" and he became convinced that "E. Vincent Millay" was "really Miss Twenty Years."[10] But the promise of money and fame was tempered by disappointment. Earle's fellow judges did not concur with his views; and so "Renascence" was given no prize. Yet when *The Lyric Year* was published in November 1912, the poem received great critical acclaim, and the judges were blamed for failing to recognize its excellence. Louis Untermeyer praised it, and Arthur Davison Ficke and Witter Bynner, whose poems also appeared in *The Lyric Year,* wrote appreciatively to the unknown Maine author.

But already—in late summer—"Renascence" had produced another effect which led to decisions and actions greatly influencing the poet's future. During an evening party at the Whitehall Inn in Camden, Vincent was prevailed upon to play the piano, sing, and recite. One of the summer visitors, Miss Caroline Dow, head of the National Training School of the YWCA in New York City, upon discovering that Vincent had composed the songs and the poem—and that "Renascence" was to be published in *The Lyric Year*—suggested that Vincent apply for a scholarship at Smith or Vassar. She promised that money for other expenses would be provided. By January 1913, Vincent had decided on Vassar, but in order to be admitted she had to make up courses in spite of her solid preparation at Camden High School and the list of authors with whom she was "very well acquainted" that she sent to Miss Dow. It included Shakespeare, Tennyson, Milton, and Wordsworth.

"You Can Get Accustomed to Anything"

In early February 1913, Vincent left Camden, a country mouse eager
for new experiences in the great world of New York City, where she
attended Barnard College for one semester. She responded to the
metropolis with high spirits and irony that are evident in her letters of
this time. She was gratified by an early invitation to tea with Sara
Teasdale and by a literary evening given expressly for her by Jessie B.
Rittenhouse, secretary of the Poetry Society of America, who wrote that
all "were on the *qui vive* to meet her. Pretty, petite, not yet over the
wonder of her sudden entry upon the literary scene, she was altogether
natural and charming."[11] To be in New York then—she had attended
the epochal Armory Show the day before the Rittenhouse party—and
to meet literary lions on equal terms must have been a heady experience. She had a sense of triumph from selling "Journey" and "God's
World" to Mitchell Kennerley, who soon issued them in the *Forum*. Of
"Journey" she informed her family: "It isn't anything great, I know.
But Miss Rittenhouse says it is nothing I need be ashamed of even if it
does come after 'Renascence'. . . ." Could she live up to the reputation
"Renascence" had brought her? In view of this haunting question,
Kennerley's twenty-five dollar check must have been reassuring.

At Barnard Vincent was very successful in a writing course taught by
William T. Brewster; he called her poem "Interim" "a very remarkable
production for a girl in college" and praised her story "Barbara on the
Beach," which later appeared in *Smart Set* (November 1914). Though
exceedingly busy, she was escorted about the city on occasion by
Salomón de la Selva, a young Nicaraguan poet. With him she rode on
the old double-decker buses and took the five-cent ferry to Staten
Island, where couples could picnic, swim, walk through the woods,
or even lie "on a hill-top underneath the moon," as she wrote in
"Recuerdo." Such a ferry ride was evidently the occasion for "Recuerdo," the Spanish title delicately complimenting her Latin compan-
ion, who was becoming her admirer.[12]

In June Vincent returned to Camden and settled down to "Latin
Prose all summer," as she wrote Ficke. She was tutored for the "stiff
entrance examination in Latin writing"[13] through correspondence with
a Vassar Latin professor, Elizabeth Hazelton Haight, who became her
lifelong friend. Having accepted Ficke more or less as her mentor

during the winter, she told him, "I have gratefully absorbed into my system all you said." But she was independent, and her correspondence with her "Dear Spiritual Advisor" was not too serious; Roman candles of her pertness constantly jet their colors over her letters.

Vincent was admitted to Vassar College with the Class of 1917. Though Vassar had an excellent faculty and a dynamic spirit, the first response of Vincent, then twenty-one, was hostile, as she told Ficke: "I hate this pink-and-gray college. . . . Every morning when I awake I swear, I say, 'Damn this pink-and-gray college!'" Her maturity, her independence, and her idealism were affronted by the strictness of college rules; but she did not long retain this attitude of flaming negation. Soon the courses and other activities elicited her loyal and excellent efforts.

By the end of her sophomore year she had established herself both as writer and as actress. Each year she played two or more progressively better roles. When Vassar students presented the Pageant of Athena, "a cooperative story of women's intellectual advancement,"[14] on 11 October 1916, as part of Vassar's fiftieth anniversary celebration, Vincent entered "shyly but eagerly" as the medieval French poet Marie de France, her long auburn hair adorned with pearls,[15] to recite the *lai* of the Honeysuckle, a story of Tristram and Iseult. President Henry Noble MacCracken thought her scene "was perhaps the loveliest" in the whole pageant.[16]

When Inez Milholland, an alumna of 1909 who had become a lawyer and suffragette leader, appeared during the celebration, she was, Mac-Cracken said, "clearly the idol of the undergraduates."[17] This Amazon, famous for her "brilliant, large-featured beauty,"[18] was an immensely magnetic young woman, in private life the wife of Eugen Boissevain, a Dutchman whom she married in 1913. After her death in late 1916 memorial meetings were held throughout the country for the dramatic crusader.[19] She gave Vincent her most dynamic example of feminism in action.

Vincent filled her college years with rewarding work both creative and academic. Her courses, chiefly in literature and languages, included Latin, French, Greek, Italian, Spanish, and German. To Professor Haight, Vincent owed a permanent interest in Latin poetry. Her studies reinforced the influence of the classics upon her and insured that she would be a learned poet, more like a Milton, Shelley, or Tennyson than a Whitman or Vachel Lindsay.

Her achievements as an actress made her envision a career on the stage. She talked with a member of the Washington Square Players, and just before graduation she was elated over the possibility of acting in Milwaukee for eight weeks that summer. Her graduation was unfortunately snarled up because of certain Vassar regulations inno- cently broken. She was rusticated from the campus, and hot controversy broke out. But finally she could write, "Commencement went off beautifully . . . (Edna St. Vincent Millay A.B.!)."[20]

"Blossom Time Is Early, But No Fruit Sets On"

After college, Vincent spent two years working extremely hard for only minimal rewards. Not having been hired for the Milwaukee season, she spent the summer of 1917 at home. Then, after visiting in Connecticut, doing some poetry readings, and typing her first collec- tion of poems for Mitchell Kennerley to publish, she went to New York, again living at Miss Dow's Training Center, again much stimu- lated by the city, again going about with De la Selva. Kennerley published *Renascence and Other Poems* that fall but paid her no royalties. But Vincent made a connection with the theater which was important in the development of her career.

Hearing that an actress was needed by the Provincetown Players, she read for the ingenue part in Floyd Dell's *The Angel Intrudes* and secured it. The Provincetown Players, headed by George Cram Cook, had a playwrights' theater that gave writers a chance to create new plays *and to see them produced*[21]—but no salaries were paid.[22] Their plays repre- sented a radical challenge to the commercial theater: "Radicalism at the moment meant deeper realism than Broadway audiences were ready to face. . . . Here was . . . a theater that did more than any other to open the channel of creative play writing."[23] Dell's play opened 28 De- cember 1917 in the Playwrights' Theatre at 139 Macdougal Street deep in Greenwich Village. Vincent performed so well that the company made her a member of the group, and Dell offered her the lead in his next play, *Sweet and Twenty,* which she accepted.[24]

Meanwhile, her sister Norma had joined Vincent in New York. "You've got to have your chance, too," Vincent had written her. Now it seemed best for the Millay sisters to live in the Village (Norma was working in a loft, checking thread-gauge wires used on airplanes),[25] where rents were cheap; and in January 1918 they moved from the

National Training School to West Ninth Street and soon after to Waverly Place.

Thus Vincent came into contact with some of the most brilliant and vigorous personalities of the time in a milieu where advanced ideas were common coin and where a particular kind of Bohemian life had developed in the crooked streets with old red-brick houses that, decades earlier, had been fashionable.[26] The spirit of the Village was congenial to her, and she had opportunities there that she could have had nowhere else. In that small definite area where people lived simply, not over-whelmed by hugeness, rush, noise, and anonymity, the spirit was, in a sense, that of a village. But in a more significant sense the spirit of Greenwich Village was unlike that of the usual American village. This very difference drew young men and women to the Village and made them vehement defenders of its values. Villagers asserted that the great touchstone of the Village spirit was honesty. In the Village a person could be himself. He was not pressed into hypocritical respect for Wall Street, Main Street, the government, or Mrs. Grundy. He was not obliged to drink behind the barn or to appear in church because his absence would look bad for his family; nor did he have to disguise an interest in art or poetry, go hungry for discussion of it, or conceal his boredom with prevailing American taste and politics. The unconven-tionality so conspicuous to visitors was an expression of honest indi-vidualism that many Americans had always considered the heart of the American tradition. One might say that people came to Greenwich Village because there, as in few other places, they could be free of the dominant middle-class values. In a way, Greenwich Village was the urban obverse of Brook Farm, another attempt to gratify the artist's "utopian wish."[27]

When Millay went there, the basic Village honesty and integrity accompanied hard work, gay camaraderie, vigorous play which some-times flared into wildness, and a fierce intensification of the sense of life. Malcolm Cowley wrote: "It didn't matter that we were penniless; . . . we were continually drunk with high spirits."[28]

It would be incorrect to say that Greenwich Village converted Millay to avant-garde ways, to feminism, free thinking, Bohemianism, or political radicalism. Evidently she would not have been essentially different had she never come to the Village.[29] When she went there to live, she was nearly twenty-six years old, and she knew what she stood for. Nevertheless, the contact with young, vigorous, and radical minds in the bubbling libertarian pot of the Village provided a kind of corroboration—a strengthening into ultimate conviction, through agreement and contention—of the values that she believed in.

Millay encountered many notable writers and artists in the Village: Malcolm Cowley, Theodore Dreiser, Alfred Kreymborg, Kenneth Burke, Dorothy Day, Paul Robeson, E. E. Cummings, Hart Crane, Llewelyn Powys, John Sloan, Wallace Stevens, Susan Glaspell, Eugene O'Neill, Djuna Barnes, Edmund Wilson, and John Peale Bishop. A number of Villagers were political radicals. Max Eastman became editor of the Socialist *Masses* in 1912; Dell, soon after arriving from Chicago in 1913, joined him as associate editor; and John Reed was drawn to radicalism when reporting the Paterson silk workers' strike and the Ludlow miners' strike in 1913. Mary Heaton Vorse, of an old New England family, had also taken the strikers' side in various disputes. Millay's views were generally in accord with theirs, and there were few issues on which her stand from 1917 to 1929 would have been distinguishable from that of the Village.

According to Malcolm Cowley the Bohemians had reversed traditional opinions on several matters. (1) Only through self-expression can anyone attain to his full individuality. (2) Thus one must live intensely in the moment, regardless of decorum. (3) No obstacle to self-expression—no hindering convention or law—can be tolerated. (4) The body is not unclean; a pagan freedom of enjoyment in love should supplant former repressions. (5) One must reject social repressions that prevent children from realizing their potentialities, so that a pure, unthwarted generation can bring salvation to an outworn social order. (6) Obviously women must have freedom equal to men's. They also believed in (7) psychological readjustment, chiefly through Freudian means, and (8) escaping Puritan bondage by going to Europe or other places unspoiled by Main Street taboos.[30] These ideas, except those of salvation through the child and of psychological adjustment, were part of Millay's credo.

During her early days in the Village while they rehearsed *Sweet and Twenty*—which opened 25 January 1918—Floyd Dell was falling in love with the poet.[31] As their intimacy increased in the theater and during discussions of poetry and all the topics of the time, they were soon in the midst of an affair—a difficult, indecisive attachment, passionate, disturbing, and too filled with psychological reefs for them to reach calm harbor. Dell, with his "tireless eager intellect,"[32] probed her psyche too assiduously. Arthur Davison Ficke's sonnet "Questioning a Lady" presents Millay's interpretation of her affair with Dell:

> His infinite curiosity too much pried
> Into that darkness which was mine alone.
> Sometimes I wished that I had merely died
> Before I let him think I was "his own."
> I am nobody's own. . . .[33]

"I Was a Child, and You a Hero Grown"

In February 1918, Ficke, then a major in the United States Army, and Millay's admirer, mentor, and friend through correspondence, passed through New York carrying military dispatches to France. Dell, who had known him in Davenport, Iowa, brought him to the Millay apartment, and Ficke met the author of "Renascence" for the first time. He and Dell, the Millay sisters, and Charles Ellis, Norma's beau, had a gay, crowded little party. They found Ficke charming, but most significant was the impact that he and Vincent had upon each other. Though the encounter was brief, though Ficke was married, and though he had to sail for France very soon,[34] emotional lightning had struck; Millay was to "wear the red heart crumpled in the side" for the rest of her days.

The flaming of their passion, the quick consummation of love, and their being wrenched apart so abruptly constituted a devastating experience. Millay later admitted to Ficke: "My time, in those awful days after you went away to France, was a mist of thinking about you & writing sonnets to you.—You were spending your time in the same way, I believe.—That day before you sailed,—I shall never forget it. You were the first man I ever kissed without thinking that I should be sorry about it afterwards." She told him, too, that a sonnet he had asked about "was written both about you & about myself—we were both like that—but are not any more. The 'golden vessel of great song,' also was written to you."

The sonnet written about both of them follows:[35]

> I only know that every hour with you
> Is torture to me, and that I would be
> From your too poignant lovelinesses free!
> Rainbows, green flame, sharp diamonds, the fierce blue[36]
> Of shimmering icebergs, and to be shot through
> With lightning or a sword incessantly—
> Such things have beauty, doubtless; but to me
> Mist, shadow, silence—these are lovely too.
> There is no shelter in you anywhere;
> Rhythmic, intolerable, your burning rays
> Trample upon me, withering my breath;
> I will be gone, and rid of you, I swear:
> To stand upon the peaks of Love always
> Proves but that part of Love whose name is Death.

The sonnet, with its Pre-Raphaelite tone, expresses the protest against the pangs of passion and the binding power of her lover's "poignant lovelinesses" which was characteristic of Millay's independence: a desperate cry—"I will be gone"—wrung from her fear of utter domination. Ficke represented the greatest challenge to her determination to remain free.

"Into the golden vessel of great song" (*Collected Poems,* 573) is an attempt to sublimate this passion, which is regarded as a common thing that, consummated, will leave the poet inarticulate. If "longing alone is singer to the lute," then the poets should continue to suffer and to long for the fruit "far and high" at the top of the tree. Picked up with ease from the ground, the fruit is a mere unvalued windfall. Millay's idealism speaks here—that high romantic estimate given to a pattern of perfection not embodied in the flesh. Yet her lover is her sun; whatever idealism and absence may do for the poet, for the woman it is bitter to suffer his loss. Her passion is strong, terrible, and permanent; and she is proud that this is so—an idea expressed emphatically in "Let you not say of me when I am old" (*CP,* 580). Perhaps she took solace from foreseeing a day when this love would be gone, and he would recall

". . . that on the day you came / I was a child, and you a hero grown" (*CP,* 581). Ultimately death would take him down: "And you as well must die, beloved dust . . ." (*CP,* 579). She was still resolved to dedicate her soul to poetry: she would not renounce it "for all the puny fever and frail sweat / Of human love"; for her soul would always return to its true home, Pieria, the "Singing Mountain" of the Muses (*CP,* 583). Thus, by idealism combined with resignation, Vincent tried to shelter herself from the storm of her love for Arthur Ficke, which, it seems, assailed her more tempestuously than any other loves. Yet it would not die.

Even without her problem of love versus career, Ficke too felt the impact of pain and idealism, mixed hopelessness, agony, and exaltation. His counterpart to Millay's sonnets is his sonnet sequence "Beauty in Exile," in which their love is represented as beautiful, pathetically hopeless, and yet sublimely uplifting, far above earthly things. They both regarded their devotion as permanent, unquestionable, and untouched by other concerns.

"I Am Most Faithless When I Most Am True"

In September 1918, Millay found another outlet for her work. Walter Adolphe Roberts, editor of *Ainslee's,* determined to "make the poetry in *Ainslee's* among the best printed in the United States."[37] De la Selva told Roberts that Millay would become an important poet, so he invited her to contribute, and he published many of her poems; but, since he paid only fifty cents a line, she began to write short stories, using the pseudonym Nancy Boyd for fiction. Her work appeared in nineteen consecutive issues of *Ainslee's.*

For a year or more Roberts was among the men in love with Vincent. They were numerous, and included John Reed, Pieter Mijer, a handsome Dutch artist from the East Indies who introduced batik to America,[38] and Scudder Middleton, a romantic-looking poet who wrote antiwar, Socialist poetry.[39] According to Floyd Dell, Vincent agreed to marry him late in the summer of 1918.[40] But though she shared many of his ideas and attended the second *Masses* trial with him in October, she could never reconcile herself to the hazard of dwindling, with marriage, into domesticity and being forced to give up her writing career. Dell lost hope of happiness with her and soon married another.[41]

Whether from association with Dell or for other reasons, Millay sympathized with Socialist ideals. In 1941 she said that at the close of World War I "she had been in sympathy with the communist ideal of 'a free and equal society' but had never embraced the Communist Party. She had been 'almost a fellow-traveller with the Communist idea as far as it went along with the socialist idea.'"[42] She was among those radicals who asserted the right, even the duty, of the individual to resist legislation that would prevent the exercise of his rights of free expression.

Meanwhile she continued her activities that fall at the Playwrights' Theatre—but work at the Provincetown brought no income, and she tried another theatrical possibility, joining the new Theatre Guild and appearing during April 1919 in Benavente's *The Bonds of Interest,* which hung on for only four weeks.[43] Though she was turning out her "Nancy Boyd" stories for income, her chief satisfaction lay in poetry. During early summer 1919, she worked on "Ode to Silence." In the fall she and Norma acted again in the Provincetown productions, and in November she announced to her mother that she had finished *Aria da Capo*—"You know the one, Pierrot & Columbine & the shepherds & the spirit of Tragedy. . . . Norma is going to play Columbine, & Charlie one of the shepherds." She herself directed the play, which she had conceived three years earlier.[44] It was the most distinguished offering of the Provincetown's 1919–20 season, and it presently took its place as an important contribution to American poetic drama.

Early in 1920 Millay wrote to a friend: "I am so tired these days— working terribly, terribly hard. . . ." She was giving readings from her poetry, she had three books ready to publish, and she was gratified by the popularity of *Aria da Capo,* which had already been put on by several little theaters and published in *Reedy's Mirror.* To Miss Rittenhouse she reported: "I find myself suddenly famous, Jessie, dear. . . . There is scarcely a little theatre or literary club in the country, so far as I can see, that isn't going to produce it or give a reading of it." Also, Edmund Wilson, already interested in her work, fell in love with her and joined the array of her suitors, as did his friend and associate at *Vanity Fair,* John Peale Bishop. Small wonder that, with her writing, directing, increased correspondence, readings, preparing books for publication, and the amorous shocks of her personal life, she was "having a sort of nervous break-down," as she announced on 7 April to Allan Ross Macdougall.

Though she was now blasé about the men who were ardently courting her, she was interested enough to invite Edmund Wilson for a weekend at Truro on Cape Cod, where the four Millays had moved for a summer of sea-winds and sun. He formally proposed as they sat, tormented by mosquitoes, in a swing on the porch. She told him she would think it over. Next morning when they were walking on the beach, Millay stared with her usual intensity at a lone egg that a gull had laid on the sand. Wilson later commemorated the experience in his poem "Provincetown,"[45] and in his novel *I Thought of Daisy* the narrator says that Rita Cavanaugh the poet (modeled on Millay) "had been listening with that odd tension which she seemed to apply to everything. . . ."[46] The determined, desert loneliness of her life impressed Wilson; never for long, apparently, would she venture within the bounds of conventional expectation but had to follow her chosen track—not without pain. The intensity with which she lived every experience devoured her energies and left her prey to illness. Her thirtieth birthday not far off, she did not wish to eliminate the possibility of marriage; yet she did not wish to marry any of the Village "lads." Nor was she sanguine that the theoretical freedom of an extramarital ménage would endure in practice without jealousy and unhappiness.[47]

Back in New York she was elated that *Vanity Fair* was featuring her work and that she received a prize of $100 from *Poetry* for "The Bean-Stalk." She was exasperated with Kennerley, however, who would neither publish her books nor communicate with her. Characteristic of her generation in the 1920s, she was not impressed by the Harding-Cox election; most intellectuals then were cynically indifferent to public affairs.

A bit later, pulled down again by illnesses, she was glad to take the opportunity to leave New York when Frank Crowninshield, editor of *Vanity Fair,* proposed that she go to Europe on a regular salary, free to write what she pleased, under either her own name or her *nom de plume,*

Nancy Boyd.[48] Just before Christmas she told her mother that ". . . my poetry . . . needs fresh grass to feed on. I am becoming sterile here. . . ." She sailed for France on the *Rochambeau,* 4 January 1921. From then until February 1923, her itinerary included stays in Paris and other French towns, England, Rome, Albania, Vienna, and Budapest.

Like most travelers, Millay at first felt keenly the emotion created by places with romantic traditions and the excitement of seeing new things. Later, her emotions became tempered by familiarity and illness, and she often felt lonely. Even in Europe she still had her living to earn. Besides her *Vanity Fair* pieces, she wrote a play, *The Lamp and the Bell,* for the Vassar alumnae, and in September she was hoping to finish her "long sonnet sequence about the New England woman," having completed "The Ballad of the Harp-Weaver"—but she wrote little poetry during this fallow year.

At jazz parties and in the cafés of Montparnasse Millay encountered other Americans visiting Europe, as they passed through, and for a while she was one of the "Dirty Four" "hard-working, Paris-mad, / Eager, blasé, young imbeciles"—"Henry and Stan and me and you" whom she commemorated in "To S. V. B.—June 15, 1940."[49] But it does not seem that she made contact with very many Europeans (though we hear of a dinner that Brancusi cooked for her at his studio) or that her European sojourn provided her with the intellectual excitement that some of her younger compatriots experienced. Among friends in the Village reports circulated later about love affairs she had in Europe. The most serious of them was with a young Frenchman, a violinist, whose parents objected to his marrying her. According to Floyd Dell, having become pregnant, she went to England without telling the violinist of her pregnancy, and had an abortion.[50] The pain of this love experience is probably reflected in "The Cameo" and "To a Musician" (*CP,* 246, 257).

In the fall of 1921 she made a four-week sally into primitive Albania, where she was again overcome by love for Ficke, and wrote: "Why aren't you here? Oh, why aren't you here? . . . I tell you I must see you again.—" Back in Rome she had conferences with Sinclair Lewis, who was scouting manuscripts for Alfred Harcourt, about *Hardigut,* a projected novel;[51] but in December, to save money, she was living in a

cheap, dreadful place on the Floragasse in Vienna. She is said to have
lived for a time with Griffin Barry, a British journalist, but was "bailed
out" by a $500 check that Ficke had his father send to her.[52]

Then another possibility of marriage suddenly arose. The proposal
came, but not directly, from Witter Bynner. But because his letter had
been lost, the only inkling she had of the proposal was the implication
in a note from Ficke with a postscript by Bynner. In a pleasant and,
naturally, rather cautious letter of 23 December, she agreed to marry
him: the idea of marrying him was not new to her. For two months,
while she was in Vienna and Budapest, they had a seriocomic correspondence over marriage and eventually decided not to marry. Meanwhile, she took in gallant stride the news that though Ficke was now
divorced, he had fallen in love with another girl.

Her perspective changed on 1 March 1922, when she received a $500
advance on *Hardigut* from Horace Liveright. Millay immediately ac-
tualized her dream of giving her mother a trip to Europe. A month later
Mrs. Millay came, and they were together for several months in Paris,
England, and the south of France, where Vincent was supposed to
finish (actually to write) *Hardigut*. Her energies depleted by illness,
however, she was not able to do so; the novel remained unwritten, and
she and her mother returned to New York in February 1923.[53]

". . . Such a Man as Any Wife
Would Pass a Pretty Lad For"

By 1923 Millay had several books to her credit, and her reputation
was growing. Frank Shay, a Village publisher, persuaded her to let him
issue *A Few Figs from Thistles* in 1920. After much delay Kennerley
published a volume of more serious poems, *Second April,* in 1921.
During 1922 Millay became a member of a group of poets who
sponsored *American Poetry: A Miscellany,* a cooperative venture started
in 1920 as a biennial volume. Millay used her space in the *Miscellany* for
eight sonnets.[54] She also issued her *Ballad of the Harp-Weaver* as a
pamphlet.

She and Edwin Arlington Robinson had been finalists for the
Pulitzer Prize for poetry in 1922; his *Collected Poems* had received the

prize over her *Few Figs.* In 1923 Wilbur L. Cross, chairman of the Pulitzer jury in poetry, and the other members put her poetry in competition again, plus the eight sonnets in *American Poetry.* Cross thought her poems represented "the best verse published in 1922," and she received the Pulitzer Prize for poetry in 1923.[55] She was the first woman to receive it.

In New York again Millay found herself exhausted and still afflicted by illness—either from aftereffects of the abortion or from intestinal difficulties. But during the spring she made a weekend visit to Croton-on-Hudson with her friend Esther Root. At Croton, then a sort of "suburb of Washington Square,"[56] a group of liberals and radicals had made homes along Mount Airy Road: Max Eastman, Eugen Boissevain, Boardman Robinson, Floyd Dell, Stuart Chase, and Dudley Field Malone. Millay attended a party given by Malone, defender of suffragists, and Doris Stevens, militant suffragist author. According to Jean Gould, Dell, Millay, and Ficke created a scenario for an impromptu play during which a couple were to fall in love. Boissevain and Millay played the couple, and while they were acting they actually did fall in love.[57]

Handsome, powerful, and boisterous, a forty-three-year-old widower once married to Inez Milholland, Boissevain was the son of a Dutch newspaper owner and an Irish mother. An athlete, he had rowed in the Henley Regatta; given to frank expression, he developed "the art of casually blurting out . . . the intimate truth" after being psychoanalyzed by Jung. He handled details of Marconi's enterprises and became a New York importer of sugar, cotton, and coffee; but he was imaginative, enjoyed being with creative people, and was a dedicated advocate of feminism.[58] Loving and pitying the poet, this big protective man took Millay, very ill the day after the party, into his house to nurse her. He assumed responsibility for seeing that she had the systematic medical attention she needed, and Dell thought that his devoted care perhaps saved her life.[59]

Millay's fatigue and illness continued. But on 30 May she announced to her mother that she loved Eugen Boissevain and was going to marry him. "There!!!" Boissevain took her to doctors who advised an operation; it was appointed for 18 July. That morning Boissevain decided that she must enter the hospital as his wife; accordingly, a justice of the peace was summoned, they were married, and in the afternoon they drove to a New York hospital.

During that summer of illness and convalescence from the operation, Millay made an adaptation of Molnar's play *Heavenly and Earthly Love* (under the title of *Launzi*). Arthur Ficke, who had already helped her escape from her unprofitable relation with Kennerley and make a permanent connection with Harper and Brothers,[60] "did a great deal of work" helping her ready *The Harp-Weaver and Other Poems* for the press. On 20 August she dictated to him her sonnet "I see so clearly now my similar years": "She had never put a word of it on paper before, but had composed it entirely in her head, as she often does."[61]

On 18 November, Millay participated in the final ceremony arranged by the National Woman's party to commemorate the seventy-fifth anniversary of the Equal Rights meeting in 1848 at Seneca Falls. In the Crypt of the Capitol, Washington, D.C., a statue was unveiled in honor of Lucretia Mott, Susan B. Anthony, and Elizabeth Cady Stanton, and Millay read her sonnet "The Pioneer." Thus after receiving the Pulitzer Prize, Millay began performing duties to which she was called as a public figure.

She went on a reading tour to the Middle West during January and February 1924, one of many such tours she was to undertake. She found them difficult and irritating, but she endured this one to earn money to pay debts and help her mother. In succeeding years her husband generally accompanied her, and in 1924 she was buoyed up by the prospect of a trip to the Orient.

The Boissevains left San Francisco for Honolulu on a Japanese ship about 19 April 1924.[62] Actually they went clear on around the world, and Millay's letters during the tour are usually exuberant with appreciation of tropical beauty, foreign scenery and customs, and returning health. But only a few of her poems appear to have a connection with these travels: "For Pao-Chin, a Boatman on the Yellow Sea" (*CP*, 218), "To a Calvinist in Bali" (*CP*, 329), Sonnet 31 of *Fatal Interview*, Sonnets 7 and 8 of "Epitaph for the Race of Man," and "The Parsi Woman" (*CP*, 506).

Since Boissevain cared little for his importing business, he was agreeable to buying a 700-acre, run-down farm in the Berkshire foothills at Austerlitz, New York, to which he and his wife moved in June 1925, and which became their base of operations for the rest of their lives. They named it "Steepletop" for a showy pink flower abounding in their meadows.

Having been commissioned by the Metropolitan to compose an opera, Deems Taylor approached the poet for a libretto. She agreed to write it, and almost until Christmas she struggled with a libretto on the story of Snow White and the Seven Dwarfs.[63] She had a constant headache, and she complained of people who kept requesting readings, autographs, advice about writing, and the like. Fame and publicity were apparently bringing their disadvantages. Finally she scrapped what she had written and took up a story of tenth-century England from the *Gesta Regum Anglorum* of William of Malmesbury. She sent the libretto of *The King's Henchman* scene by scene to Deems Taylor, who composed a piano score and later completed the orchestration in Paris.[64]

She found time also to send, over the signature of Nancy Boyd, a satirical poem called "The Armistice Day Parade" to Franklin P. Adams's column "The Conning Tower." The poem resulted from a concern over growing militarism; it illustrates the antiwar sentiments of many liberals in the 1920s:

> "I shall not march," said the Major,
> In the Armistice Day parade."
> . . . .
> "If you went and abolished war," said he,
> "Where in hell would the army be?"[65]

Millay completed the final revisions of the proofs of the libretto with Arthur Ficke's help in Santa Fe, where the Fickes were then living. She sent them off 6 December. The premiere of *The King's Henchman* occurred on 17 February 1927, a memorable production of a brilliant American opera in English with a poetic quality most unusual in a libretto. Highly successful both at the Metropolitan and on the road, *The King's Henchman* went through three printings in three weeks, and by November was in its eighteenth printing. Millay had reached another crest of success and fame.[66]

"Justice Denied"

In the summer of 1927 the Sacco-Vanzetti case stirred indignant liberals the world over. Nicola Sacco and Bartolomeo Vanzetti, Italians and anarchists both, had been arrested, tried, and convicted of murder and robbery of a paymaster and his guard, a crime committed 15 April 1920 at South Braintree, Massachusetts. It was widely felt that the Italians were victims of postwar antiradical hysteria and of the prejudice of Judge Webster Thayer. For six years their lawyers had staved off their execution. In late 1926, Governor Fuller of Massachusetts was urged to appoint a committee to reinvestigate the case.[67]

The governor was petitioned for a stay of execution and an order for an investigation, and affidavits were filed alleging prejudice on the part of Judge Thayer.[68] Fuller started an investigation and on 1 June appointed an advisory committee of three, who submitted a report to the governor on 27 July. Fuller announced on 3 August that the report tallied with the result of his own investigation: Sacco and Vanzetti were guilty and must die.[69] The decision created a "world stir" the next day. Defense attorneys protested the secrecy of the inquiry; protest meetings were held; in France, Henry Wadsworth Dana, "an American, who recently has been prominent at French Communist gatherings," presented a motion for a twenty-four-hour general strike. Presently the American Civil Liberties Union protested.[70] Judge Thayer refused to withdraw from the hearing (before himself) on his own prejudice in the case. On 9 August he denied motions for a stay of execution; appeals, protests, and world-wide demonstrations had no effect; but the governor issued a reprieve until 22 August.[71] On 20 August, Boston sympathizers sent out a wire: "Picketers urgently needed to picket State House beginning Saturday morning until the execution of Sacco and Vanzetti. It is all we can do now. Will you come and bring anyone you can for that service."[72] To this appeal Millay responded. If she had not been concerned over Sacco and Vanzetti in 1920–21, she had been concerned over weakening of libertarian tradition, as her poem "To the Liberty Bell" attests:

> Toll, toll.
>
> Yet toll not.
> Lest to our shame we learn how few today
> Would stand in the street and listen.[73]

As hopes for the condemned men grew more desperate, Millay put into Ruth Hale's hands her poem "Justice Denied in Massachusetts" written "as her contribution to the registering of the feeling many of us have. . . ." Miss Hale (Heywood Broun's wife) sent the poem to the *New York Times,* where it was printed 22 August. Millay's feeling that under the cloud of injustice the precious American inheritance was blighted, never to grow again, must have been shared by many.

On Sunday, 21 August, the whole Boston police force and the militia were called out; the traditional use of Boston Common for speeches was denied; and picketers were arrested.[74] The execution was to be immediately after midnight of 22 August, and on that day Millay and her husband were in Boston with thousands of others. Across the Common from the State House a continual protest meeting was being held at Scenic Temple: groups of a dozen or so people would leave to picket the State House, only to be arrested. While members of the American Legion uttered catcalls and hisses, picketers bearing placards and banners marched in single file to the State House; police warned them that they were "sauntering and loitering" and after seven minutes hauled them in patrol wagons to the Joy Street Station. Near the head of a group of of thirteen writers Millay marched carrying a placard with the inscription "If these men are executed, justice is dead in Massachusetts."

A photograph shows Millay and the poet Lola Ridge being conducted in the searing heat to a patrol wagon. Both women wear grimly set faces, dour and downcast. More than 150 picketers were arrested and taken to "the huge, bare, dusty room where the court sat. . . . We were all huddled in together," Katherine Anne Porter wrote, "and stood around, or sat on the grimy floor or on a shallow flight of steps. . . . Big, overmuscled, beefy policemen with real thug faces bawled at us senselessly. . . ."[75] They were finally bailed out at $25 each. Boissevain posted bail for Millay, and they put up bail for others.

That afternoon Millay had an audience with Governor Fuller and told him how two men accused of murder in Maine were convicted and hanged because the governor would not intercede. Later the murderer confessed. Governor Fuller said he would think about what she had told him. Late in the evening she composed a final appeal, which was delivered to the State House at 11:40. In her eloquent letter Millay wrote:

You promised me, and I believed you truly, that you would think of what I said. I exact of you that promise now. . . .

I cry to you with a million voices: answer our doubt. Exert the clemency which your high office affords.

There is need in Massachusetts of a great man tonight. It is not yet too late for you to be that man.

But Fuller remained silent, and Sacco and Vanzetti were executed shortly after midnight.[76]

Millay and five others refused to pay a $10 fine, and appealed. Though she went again to Boston in October, the trial was postponed. The defendants were acquitted 3 December 1927.[77] Meanwhile on 25 August the *New York World* printed a letter by Edmund Pearson showing errors in the story she had told Fuller. In her reply of 6 October she demonstrated that Pearson too had made errors—all the errors indicating how easily people can be mistaken, governors included.[78]

Millay then wrote her article "Fear," which was published in the *Outlook* on 9 November 1927. She asserted that the young saw through the hypocrisies of their elders. The war had disillusioned them: "they are beginning to understand why you went to war; they have seen you engaged in many another dubious and embarrassing activity; and now they have seen this." As for herself, in her bitterness even death might be a comfort; she was dismayed by "the ugliness of man, his cruelty, his greed, his lying face." These bitter opinions were the accepted views of radicals who thought that the United States had entered the war for materialistic reasons and who were affronted and alarmed by A. Mitchell Palmer's Red-hunt, the union-smashing of big business, vigilante terrorizing by the Ku Klux Klan, and loud-pedaling of "100 per cent Americanism."[79] Such views appeared unpatriotic to many *Outlook* readers, but Millay was comforted by a letter from Bynner and by her husband's support.

The Sacco-Vanzetti case made Millay's social consciousness more specific; she became, as she told Grace King in 1941, "more aware of the underground workings of forces alien to true democracy." The affair increased her scorn for the American public and deepened her disillusionment with mankind.[80]

"A House on Upland Acres"

At Steepletop the poet had a refuge against vulgar encroachment upon her creative hours and against the shocks of worldly encounters. The new owners gradually turned the remote, run-down farm into a modest chateau. Boissevain assumed all workaday responsibilities, exercising the functions of husband, lover, farm overseer, business manager, secretary, and at times a staff of servants. When they were unable to get, or to retain, servants, he cooked and attended to other household matters with no loss of equanimity.[81] He formulated a model philosophy for the mate of a woman of genius: her poetic task was "to immortalize the beauty of the moment," and consequently "she must ever remain open to contact with life's intensities." He solved their problem by managing all the "quotidian matters" because "it is so obvious that Vincent is more important than I am."[82] Thus Vincent's once-persistent problem of career versus marriage was resolved by this union in which the husband, not insisting on traditional prerogatives but putting her career foremost in their lives, allowed her all possible freedom—even sexual freedom, for like typical Villagers the Boissevains gave love, wherever it might flare up, precedence over possessiveness or adherence to vows.[83] Apparently children were not a necessity in their marriage.[84] So Vincent was fortunate to find in Eugen such a haven, for none of her other lovers, the creative, intellectual men, was capable of the self-abnegating devotion that her husband gave her, both out of love and on principle.

Her privacy and freedom for writing assured, Millay could retire at will to her upstairs study to create poems in her ten-cent notebooks; then, to relieve tension, come down at times to work in flower gardens or to play the piano. But she longed for the sea, so they spent some summer weeks in Maine each year; and after the summer of 1933, when they bought Ragged Island in Casco Bay, they had a salt-water hideaway.[85] Still they maintained cordial relations with a good many friends and entertained, sometimes on a large scale, from time to time. Millay was also glad to help other writers as her strength permitted: writing recommendations for Stephen Vincent Benét, E. E. Cummings, and Kay Boyle; advising Abbie Huston Evans on the publication of her poems; writing a detailed criticism of Edmund Wilson's novel *I Thought of Daisy*;[86] and generously helping Llewelyn Powys when he was under heavy expense, having been convicted for libel.[87]

Some years she went on reading tours in the fall and early winter. Late in 1928, she gave a reading at the University of Chicago for the benefit of the University Poetry Club; George Dillon, who had graduated the year before and was on the staff of *Poetry,* introduced her to the large, enthusiastic audience. He was deeply impressed by her appearance and performance—her hair, "true reddish gold," contrasting with her "flowing robe, aquamarine velvet, with a train, which gave her an illusion of height"; and her voice, "a rich music, a diapason ranging from tragic to gay effects, that was unlike any other. . . . I thought her voice the most affecting I had ever heard." He also thought that the glamour of the brilliantly successful occasion "was responsible for the rapport which then established itself between us." They became further acquainted at a gathering afterwards. "For my part, I was permanently won,"[88] he wrote.

Dillon's ingenuous statement is true in more ways than one. Millay's heart, it seems, succumbed immediately to the fascination of the young man, and the next day she handed him a copy of the poem, written on the back of a telegram, that became Sonnet 2 of *Fatal Interview.* Millay initiated the affair; whether or not it took precisely the course of the one delineated in *Fatal Interview,* they became lovers—Millay nearing thirty-seven and Dillon only twenty-two—and Dillon was the man behind the love sonnets of *Fatal Interview.* If one may assume that *Fatal Interview* generally conforms to their affair, it seems likely that it flourished and then diminished during 1929 and early 1930, for Sonnets 26, 45, and 46 of *Fatal Interview* were published in *Poetry* for October 1930 (along with Dillon's sonnet sequence "Address to the Doomed"), and 24 other of the sonnets were published in various periodicals before *Fatal Interview* came out on 15 April 1931. But the affair was not over; it continued, at least sporadically, for several more years. Millay and Dillon lived together in Paris during the winter and spring of 1932, when he had a Guggenheim grant and she was buying clothes at Boulanger (cf. "The Fitting"; *CP,* 342); at other times, probably also while the poets were collaborating on their translation of Baudelaire, they had a *ménage à trois* with the reluctant Eugen, who as "troubled lord" uneasily acquiesced, confronted by a rival nearly thirty years younger. But though Boissevain feared his wife might leave him, she did not, and their lives eventually settled down, it appears, into more or less their former pattern.

Dillon, who was a modest and not particularly assertive man, felt, according to his cousin Alice Baur Hodges, that he was "being devoured"; caught between Millay and his mother (who disapproved of the affair)—"two very strong women"—he was in a difficult situation. But, whatever their personal entanglements, he and Millay honestly admired each other as poets.[89]

The publication of Millay's books continued (after *The King's Henchman* her greatest success was *Fatal Interview*); during the 1930s she spent some 20 percent of her time in travel, and new honors kept coming to her. Yet death could cause deep grief: Elinor Wylie was cut down on 16 December 1928; further sadness came with the death of Mrs. Millay on 5 February 1931—her burial took place at Steepletop a week later—;[90] and Henry Tolman Millay died in Bangor, 19 December 1935.[91]

Millay's association with Dillon was professional as well as personal, and in 1934–35 they produced a translation of Baudelaire's *Flowers of Evil*. He showed her some translations he had made, and she, having urged him to publish a book of them, agreed to his joking proposal that she write a preface for it. Then she soon became absorbed herself in translating, and while Dillon visited at Steepletop in the summer of 1935, she completed numerous translations and wrote part of a preface. In September the Boissevains went to France, where Millay did some research on Baudelaire and consulted with her friend Lucie Delarue-Mardrus, a poet and novelist. Back in New York on 13 October, she busied herself at Steepletop and in Florida till past New Year's with details of the book.

"The Whole Round World Rolling in Darkness"

Millay then concentrated on *Conversation at Midnight* and finished it by May 1936. But when, shortly after arriving at Sanibel Island, she looked up from the beach and saw the Palms Hotel in flames, she knew that she had lost the manuscript of her new book. At Steepletop she struggled to set the poems down again, as accurately as she could.

During that summer other troubles began. She pitched out of a station-wagon when the door accidentally flew open, injured her back, suffered pain for years, and, in fact, was involved with doctors and operations until late 1941. Floyd Dell heard reports that during these years she became a morphine addict but then accomplished the "heroic feat" of breaking the habit completely.[92] In the 1930s and 1940s she and Eugen were also in the habit of drinking regularly, probably no more than their neighbors did, but Max Eastman thought that they drank too much and that "chemical stimulation blunted the edge of Edna's otherwise so carefully cherished genius."[93] At any rate, her peace of mind and her principles were also subjected to great stress. She was disturbed by the Spanish Civil War, by the increasing Nazi-Fascist encroachments on liberty, by the growing certainty of general war, its eruption, and, finally, American participation in it.

In 1941 Millay told Grace King: "Eight years ago I was an ardent pacifist, a true conscientious objector. My thought and opinion were that it was wrong to go to arms."[94] But the failure of the League of Nations to prevent Japan's attack on China and Italy's conquest of Ethiopia, the Nazi dismemberment and succeeding occupation of Czechoslovakia, and the German-Russian nonaggression treaty of 23 August 1939 changed Millay's outlook and finally convinced her "that no course of action other than the sternest resistance" was possible.[95] Like millions of other Americans, she gradually abandoned her antiwar attitude and advocated preparedness.

After the Germans smashed the Low Countries and France in May and June 1940, she threw herself into writing propaganda poetry for preparedness and the cause of the Allies. Once the United States declared war, she cooperated with the Writers' War Board to produce propaganda verse, although she knew that it was inferior and she feared that her reputation as a poet might be destroyed by it. At last ill health and the strain of writing propaganda against deadlines overcame her. She suffered a nervous breakdown in 1944 and for a long time was unable to write at all.

She received further honors; but a number of dear friends died during these years: Llewelyn Powys in 1939; her sister Kathleen and Eugene Saxton, her editor at Harper, in 1943; John Peale Bishop in 1944; and, on 30 November 1945, Arthur Davison Ficke. She must have felt more and more lonely and dependent upon her husband.

After 1945, she was able to begin writing again and took even more pains than usual to polish her poems, for she had grown more critical from her unhappy experience of writing propaganda "—from the point of view of poetry, sloppy, garrulous, and unintegrated. . . ."

One afternoon in August 1948, Edmund Wilson called at Steepletop; he had not seen Vincent for nineteen years and was shocked at her changed appearance, her extreme nervousness, and the way in which Eugen babied her. Wilson felt that they were living in a sort of backwater of the past; and both Max Eastman and Harrison Dowd believed that they were ill-advised to isolate themselves as much as they did.[96] Perhaps Eugen was overprotective of his wife; it may be that because he shielded her too much, her abilities declined and she had less "creative tension so necessary to the serious artist."[97] On the other hand, Joan Dash says that Eugen urged her to work very hard at her poetry in the postwar years, and she believes that his care enabled Millay to create poetry again, the only activity that gave life meaning for her.[98]

Nearing seventy, Boissevain wrote to Gustav Davidson on 22 August 1949: "I have been terribly busy, too busy with haying with insufficient help, to attend to my correspondence."[99] Eight days later he was dead. After X-ray examinations in Albany, doctors in Boston found that he had cancer of the right lung. The lung was removed; he rallied, seemed to be recovering, then suffered a stroke and died 30 August 1949.

After his funeral Millay apparently drank recklessly, would not eat properly, and had to enter Doctors' Hospital. But she was determined to return home on 24 September and although solicitous friends opposed her decision, she had her way, and with a sensible regime of rehabilitation soon regained health. Stoically enduring her grief, she passed a lonely year at Steepletop. Her professional interests quickly reasserted themselves, and in correspondence about her work she was her usual tough-minded self. She was accumulating poems and expected to produce another book. But the volume, when published, was the posthumous *Mine the Harvest.*

Vincent died at Steepletop of a heart attack; she was alone, sitting on the stairs, on that night of 19 October 1950.

Chapter Two

"All That Once Was I!"

Renascence and Other Poems

"Renascence," the most salient poem in Millay's first volume, conveys with extraordinary freshness and with generally fine technique a sense of the immense mystery of the universe. Like much of her poetry, it is in the tradition of American transcendentalism. "Interim" and "The Suicide" are ambitious pieces of apprentice work that reflect the encounter of late adolescence with problems of death, duty, and world-design. Aspects of the poet's genius later to be much more fully demonstrated are revealed in other poems of the book: the intense, observant worshiper of beauty, and the girl who, in sonnets and brief lyrics, catches the nuances of feminine loves and sorrows.

"Renascence" (*CP,* 3–13), a substantial work (214 lines) in tetrameter couplets, falls into four sections. The introductory section (lines 1–28) emphasizes the limitations of the evironment and the desire to reach out to freedom. But for the as yet undeveloped soul, the sky itself is "not so grand," only an arm-length above: "And reaching up my hand to try, / I screamed to feel it touch the sky." The great identification-experience of the second section (lines 29–102) is then developed, from the pressing down of Infinity upon the poet and the holding of a glass before her "shrinking sight" "Until it seemed I must behold / Immensity made manifest," through the consequent awareness of the workings of the Universe and the suffering of all the world's pain and sin, to the capitulation, death, and sinking into the grave of the "tortured soul." In the third section (lines 103–80), with the falling of rain upon the grave, the poet gradually feels again a longing for life and beauty that is finally voiced in the vehement prayer "O God, I cried, give me new birth, / And put me back upon the earth!" The grave is washed away by a torrent of rain, the senses are restored, and the poet is reborn: "I breathed my soul back into me." The fourth and last division (lines 181–214), like the first, is short; it expresses exultant joy in earthly beauty, and even deeper rapture in the new knowledge of God, and the conclusion that the experience justifies: "The world stands out on either side / No wider than the heart is wide; / Above the world is stretched the sky,— / No higher than the soul is high."

"Renascence" opens with simple, little-girl language; then, as Louis Untermeyer wrote: "mystery becomes articulate. It is as if a child playing . . . had, in the midst of prattling, uttered some shining and terrible truth."[1] The terrifying vastness of the universe and the awesome complexity of individual forms issuing from the divine energy— "Immensity made manifold"—are represented in the second part with stimulating, specific words, as in "And brought unmuffled to my ears / The gossiping of friendly spheres, / The creaking of the tented sky, / The ticking of eternity." Such specific terms and metaphors that they imply brought praise of the poem for its remarkable freshness. The imagined situation of the finite human being taking on the omniscience of God is extremely striking. No doubt many people have toyed with this idea: "I saw and heard, and knew at last / The How and Why of all things, past, / And present, and forevermore." But to render the experience with anything like justice in some fifty lines is a large undertaking, and the poet met the challenge.

The reader is made aware of the evil of "the Universe, cleft to the core," through the metaphor of the "great wound" (which evidently is to be imagined as a gash inflicted after a deadly snake bite)–". . . and could not pluck / My lips away till I had drawn / All venom out." Then follows "infinite remorse of soul." Though the poem contains many examples of effective run-on lines, the enjambment is especially fine in the succeeding passage, the stresses falling on the key words:

> All sin was of my sinning, all
> Atoning mine, and mine the gall
> Of all regret. Mine was the weight
> Of every brooded wrong, the hate
> That stood behind each envious thrust,
> Mine every greed, mine every lust.

The passing from the "all" to the "every" is particularly intense, as expressed in examples of death by fire, of starvation, of shipwreck—

when "A thousand screams the heavens smote; / And every scream tore through my throat." Then the poem returns to the general: hurt and death create compassion; but in fact it is the blended elements of godhead, omnisentience plus love, justice, and pity: "All suffering mine, and mine its rod; / Mine, pity like the pity of God—" that prove too much for the "finite Me." For how can one—especially when young, at the threshold of adult years—face such a world? Better to die than to participate in a world so poisoned with suffering and sin. At last the "anguished spirit" is free; the poet sinks into the earth and enjoys the peace of death.

Then upon the silent, lonely grave there falls the "pitying rain": "I lay and heard each pattering hoof / Upon my lowly, thatchèd roof. . . ." And the poet develops greater love for the "friendly sound" of the rain—indeed, for all the "multi-colored, multi-form, / Belovèd beauty" of earth. All through this section the poet uses alliteration boldly and varies the iambic foot with great vigor and success, especially in relation to run-on lines:

> To drink into my eyes the shine
> Of every slanting silver line,
> To catch the freshened, fragrant breeze
> From drenched and dripping apple-trees
> . . . .
> Until the world with answering mirth
> Shakes joyously, and each round drop
> Rolls, twinkling, from its grass-blade top.

After the prayer—"And let the heavy rain, down-poured / In one big torrent, set me free—" the answer comes in terms of several implied metaphors: the "rush / Of herald wings," "the vibrant string / Of my ascending prayer," "the startled storm-clouds reared on high"—until at the tremendous climax, the feeling heightened with heavy alliteration, spondaic feet, and assonance, ". . . the big rain in one black wave / Fell from the sky and struck my grave."

After this crashing crescendo and a dramatic pause, the poem resumes *pianissimo*—"I know not how such things can be,"— explaining how the senses of smell, hearing, and feeling return; and then, climactically, comes the sense of sight:

> And all at once the heavy night
> Fell from my eyes and I could see!
> A drenched and dripping apple-tree,
> A last long line of silver rain,
> A sky grown clear and blue again.

The enjambment preceding *fell* gives the word a great force at just the right place; just right, too, are the three lines that follow: each contains a separate observation going from small to large and each has its distinctive alliteration. With beauty and sweetness, "a miracle / Of orchard-breath," the soul returns.

The joy that follows is emphasized with dramatic inversion: "Ah! Up then from the ground sprang I / And hailed the earth with such a cry / As is not heard save from a man / Who has been dead, and lives again." The Lazarus-ecstasy is quickly modulated to adoration and confidence; the soul reborn is also re-formed, or transformed:

> O God, I cried, no dark disguise
> Can e'er hereafter hide from me
> Thy radiant identity!
> Thou canst not move across the grass
> But my quick eyes will see Thee pass. . . .
> . . . .
> God, I can push the grass apart
> And lay my finger on Thy heart!

The experience has been apocalyptic. In spite of dark disguises (the evil shot through the world), God is everywhere. The poet's feeling of renewed certainty resembles that of Adam, who, "recall'd / To life prolong'd," was assured by Michael of God's omnipresence: "and of his presence many a signe / Still following thee" (*Paradise Lost,* 11:330–31, 351–52). The poet concludes from her experience that life is not to be estimated in terms of material environment: the dimensions of one's life are commensurate with heart-breadth (sympathy) and soul-height (spiritual elevation).

Although the poem is in the transcendentalist tradition of Emerson and Whitman, the simplicity and mysticism of "Renascence" made readers think of Blake and Coleridge. In a letter to Ficke, Millay denied that she had imitated "The Ancient Mariner"—"And I never even heard of William Blake." She strongly emphasized her independence as a poet: "I never get anything from a book. I see things with my own eyes. . . ."

Harriet Monroe praised "Renascence" highly.[2] Minot was impressed by "the quick rush of metaphors."[3] Another effective device is parallelism; the repetition and near-repetition of lines and key terms, as if they were musical motifs, give the poem a resemblance to a symphony. Technically, the writing is accomplished. Since the danger of sing-song monotony in iambic tetrameter couplets is notorious, Millay took a considerable risk in using the measure; she invited comparison, for example, with Milton's "L'Allegro" and "Il Penseroso," Marvell, and Emerson. Her work, sensitively varied in rhythm, in enjambment, and in the placing of the caesura, endures the comparison very well.

If "Renascence" owes anything to the example of other poets, they are probably Marvell and Browning. When at Barnard, Millay wrote to Ficke: "You didn't know that Andrew Marvel [sic] is an old love of mine and that his *Coy Mistress* is one of my favorites." Line 116 of "Renascence," "A grave is such a quiet place," reminds one of Marvell's "The grave's a fine and private place"; and there is something of Marvell's metaphysical tone in lines 29–44. Browning's "Easter-Day" also recounts an apocalyptic experience; the speaker becomes aware of the world on the verge of Judgment Day—". . . the utmost walls / Of time, about to tumble in / And end the world—" (XV), and he boldly chooses the world—"It was so beautiful, so near / Thy world. . . .

> Nor did I refuse
> To look above the transient boon
> Of time; but it was hard so soon
> As in a short life, to give up
> Such beauty: I could put the cup
> Undrained of half its fulness, by;
> But to renounce it utterly,
> —That was too hard!   (XVI)

The feeling resembles that in "Renascence"; Browning's poem differs from Millay's in having a debate between the human speaker and God, who scornfully allows him all the opulence of earth and "its shows."

The speaker finally rejects earth, hoping to reach "the Better Land!" "Then did the Form expand, expand— / I knew Him through the dread disguise . . ." (XXXII). The phrasing is close to Millay's "dark disguise," and there are some similarities in versification, particularly in Section XV of "Easter-Day." Both poems use iambic tetrameter couplets with a good deal of repetition, alliteration, and enjambment.[4] But "Renascence" is not set up in terms of a contrast between earth and some "Better Land." The basic difference in these poems is that between Victorian orthodoxy and transcendentalist pantheism.

In a few places where Millay's diction falls to triteness, she attempts to set things right by crying out with strained vehemence. Some padding and strain are especially noticeable in lines 49–55, with "would fain pluck . . . nay! . . . Ah, fearful pawn: . . . paid I toll. . . ." She is also betrayed by the *self-elf* rhyme into the fatuousness of lines 161–62: "A sound as of some joyous elf / Singing sweet songs to please himself." Another weakness is what Edward Davison called the "girlish pretty-pretty-ness" of "I 'most could touch it with my hand!" But these are few and minor blemishes in a fine poem which with sense impressions of extraordinary precision ("The creaking of the tented sky, / The ticking of Eternity"); with high metaphorical voltage ("each pattering hoof" of the rain); and with a beautiful matching of sound and sense, communicates reverberantly to the imagination a tremendous yet subtle experience. Untermeyer called it "possibly the most astonishing performance of this generation"; Floyd Dell found it "comparable in its power and vision to 'The Hound of Heaven'"; and Davison said: "No girl of her age has ever written a better poem."[5]

In her first volume Millay treats a number of themes that she will return to later; the book is like an overture to her work. Both "Interim" and "The Suicide" continue the concern of "Renascence" over the ultimate design of the world. "Interim" is a blank-verse soliloquy expressing the grief of a man after the recent, unexpected death of his wife. Professor Brewster praised it for its smooth verse, its "many striking figures," and "great command of language." It contains musings about the mystery of God's purposes, a rebellious interlude, a refusal to indulge in conventional outpourings of grief or consolatory belief in immortality of the soul, and, finally, a tribute to faith: "Faith it is / That keeps the world alive." Without faith no purpose would be achieved; ". . . and the all-governing reins / Would tangle in the frantic hands of God / And the worlds gallop headlong to destruction!" (*CP*, 23). The speaker, a "modern" young man, is, like Millay, a free-thinker determined to be honest; but the poem seems derivative and inconclusive. It reminds one of dramatic monologues of Browning or Tennyson and, as Untermeyer said, "wanders off into periods of reflection and rhetoric."[6]

"The Suicide," an allegorical narrative in heroic couplets, is rather like Tennyson's "The Palace of Art," though more Pre-Raphaelite in tone. The speaker curses Life because it has inflicted work, suffering, and deprivation upon him—although "I asked of thee no favour save this one: / That thou wouldst leave me playing in the sun!" (*CP*, 26). His suicide is represented as an approach to a strange and ugly door of the house of life. Finally, admitted to his "Father's house," he has joy and no responsibility, but when "weary of . . . lonely ease," he begs for "a little task / To dignify my days," the Father refuses: " 'Thou hadst thy task, and laidst it by . . .' " (*CP*, 31). Both of these poems lack the dazzling freshness, beauty, and rapture of "Renascence."

Of the shorter pieces in the volume, practically all of which were written during Millay's college years, "God's World" conveys that rapture best and is the most impressive. It may seem old-fashioned with its use of the pathetic fallacy—the woods "that ache and sag / And all but cry with colour!"—and its *thee's* and *thy's* and *prithee*; but, after all, it is a formal address which ends with a prayer. More than any other poem, perhaps, it is characteristic of the electric personality supercharged with sensitivity that has been described by so many who knew Millay: "My soul is all but out of me,—let fall / No burning leaf; prithee, let no bird call" (*CP*, 32). The terms used—*crush, lift, cannot get thee close enough, such a passion*—suggest a sublimation of sexual feeling. Her expression of this feeling, as Miss Pettit says, "took the freedom usually associated with masculine creativity. In this respect she, as woman poet, was new."[7] Millay often deals later with the theme of almost unbearable ecstasy.

There are also poems of the broken heart, such as "Ashes of Life," which suggests the frustrations of the rejected woman and hints at rebellion as she sees herself passing through life at an unendurably petty pace. In "Three Songs of Shattering," heartbreak is given symbolic expression through nature; the third song begins:

> All the dog-wood blossoms are underneath the tree!
>   Ere spring was going,—ah, spring is gone!
> And there comes no summer to the likes of you and me,—
>   Blossom time is early, but no fruit sets on. (*CP*, 42)

Like "Renascence," "Sorrow" deals wth the impact of pain upon the pitying heart. Trochaic meter is handled well, and the verse-movement excellently managed in the closing lines.

With "Indifference" we find the first appearance of The Girl, a character whose true feelings contrast ironically with those that she advertises to the world. This girl self-assuredly declares that she is not eager for love; but, when Love came, "he found me at my window with my big cloak on . . ." (*CP*, 45).

Various of these poems, with their four-beat lines in duple rhythm, follow the example of Yeats in "The Lake Isle of Innisfree," and the balladlike pieces suggest early Yeats, although transposed to a feminine key. In "Witch-Wife," a lyric of three ballad stanzas, a husband describes an uncanny woman whose "voice is a string of coloured beads, / Or steps leading into the sea." He concludes that ". . . she never will be all mine" (*CP*, 46). Resistance to possession, with fierce resentment of any intrusion upon privacy and suggestions of a flight motif, is a theme that appears frequently in Millay's poetry. "Bluebeard," one of the six sonnets in *Renascence and Other Poems,* expresses her woman-independence allusively, although it is a dramatic monologue by a man who forbade the opening of one door—behind which lies only "An empty room, cobwebbed and comfortless" (*CP*, 566), suggesting a determination to keep private troubles to oneself. Millay used the theme of Bluebeard and the forbidden room several times.

Four of the six sonnets in the first volume are in the Petrarchan mode, which she used in nearly half of her published sonnets.[8] Few of these early sonnets are packed with ore; they tend to be verbose, as in "Mindful of you the sodden earth in spring," with its wordy catalogue of nature exhibits, and "Not in this chamber only at my birth," where need for rhymes induces padding: "I cried, but in strange places, steppe and firth / I have not seen, through alien grief and mirth" (*CP*, 564). Millay told Grace King in 1941 that she wrote this sonnet because she "was stirred by the outbreak of war in 1914." She called it "the blueprint of my social consciousness,"[9] identifying herself with all suffering humanity—"Child of all mothers, native of the earth." The sestet expresses world-ranging sensibilities offended by the dying of the spirit of brotherhood among mankind. This poem introduces a thought-pattern (the human condition–cultural decline–personal regret or disgust) that Millay often presented later.

In addition to "Bluebeard" the best sonnets are "Time does not bring relief," another expression of heartbreak, and "If I should learn, in some quite casual way," in which she imagines reading of the death of her lover fom another passenger's paper on a subway train. A modern rendering of the concept that a person who has suffered a terrible grief must be stricken mute,[10] it cuts quite away from nature to reflect the contemporary New York scene. Although lines 13–14 show very well the callous, vulgar world oblivious to private griefs, they should not be misjudged as flippant.

A Few Figs from Thistles

One might have thought from the deprecatory remarks of some reviewers about *A Few Figs from Thistles* that the world, the flesh, and the devil had completely taken over Millay's poetic life. They had regarded her as a mystic with "looks commercing with the skies," and now she popped up as an impudent gamine sticking out her tongue with terrible irreverence. But *A Few Figs* expressed gospel for the youth of the 1920s, who with "rash, impatient, wild ardor and insolence and cynicism"[11] were snatching at joy in the postwar years. Floyd Dell saw that these poems, which intensified the "Millay legend" of impulse and naughtiness, matched the mood of youth:

The state of the young mind is individualistic, egocentric, passionately rebellious against authority. . . . The newer mood of girlhood, that mood of freedom which is dramatized outwardly by bobbed hair, finds itself pleasantly expressed in this volume. . . .[12]

The Jazz Age was beginning, the age in which the typical writer would say he detested politics, believed only in liberty, and could best be described as an anarchist; for "on principle he would fight to the death against Prohibition, censorship, blue laws and all that sort of

thing."[13] Scott Fitzgerald spoke for the postwar generation: all through
his work run the motifs of individualism and rebellion, transiency,
excitement, and courage to follow absolutely one's own course. Millay
was presently regarded as the representative of that same generation. In
fact, Millay captured the allegiance of her generation exactly as J. D.
Salinger for much the same reasons captured that of another postwar
generation thirty years later. With the wickedly wide-eyed perversity
of the "Second Fig," the don't-give-a-damn excitement of beauty and
transiency, the intense brief experience all the more intense because—
like the famous candle of the "First Fig"—"it will not last the night,"
Millay threw down the younger-generation challenge to prudence and
respectability: "Come and see my shining palace built upon the sand"
(*CP*, 127).

Llewellyn Jones termed it a "poetry of mischief and light."[14] "The
Penitent" tells about an archly impenitent girl. The speaker in "She Is
Overheard Singing" enjoys a "true love" who is a rover, a liar, and a false
one—yet attractive to women. She exults over her neighbors who live
dull lives with dull men, for she has uncertainty and excitement in her
life. The neighbor who draws the "Portrait" is a conventional housewife
shocked by the Bohemianism of one who neglects domestic routines to
enjoy the best of the sun before doing dishes, "weeds her lazy lettuce /
By the light of the moon," and "leaves the clover standing / And the
Queen Anne's lace!" (*CP*, 142–43). Bold and unfeminine, no doubt, to
conventional minds seemed the Cavalier praise of inconstancy in
"Thursday"—an exotic in this child's garden of verse: "And why you
come complaining / Is more than I can see. / I loved you
Wednesday,—yes—but what / Is that to me?" (*CP*, 129). Hinted
approval of infidelity and experimentation also appears in "To the Not
Impossible Him."

The five sonnets of this volume, all in the Shakespearean mode—
fluent, rhythmically varied, and deftly controlled—in spite of their wit
and comparative lightness, are better than those earlier published.
"Love, though for this you riddle me with darts" (reminiscent of
Donne's "Death, be not proud") defies Love and praises freedom: "unto
no querulous care / A fool. . . ." Yet, as in other of these sonnets, there
is an element of paradox: the poet really wishes to be pierced by the
golden arrow: "(Now will the god, for blasphemy so brave, / Punish
me, surely, with the shaft I crave!)" (*CP*, 568). The final couplets,

handled in a way she learned from Shakespeare, are all effective. She
insists upon the "alterable mood" of the woman. In "I do but ask that
you be always fair," only constant beauty will insure constancy; the
man's pleading and anger will merely encourage "further vagrancy" and
"irremediable flight" (*CP,* 567). The sonnets struck a new note, for
they assume that the woman no less than the man is playing at the love
game. Millay's Cavalier air[15] shows best in "Oh, think not I am faithful
to a vow!" This has as its basis a romantic ideal: "Faithless am I save to
love's self alone." The paradox appears in the sestet and is climaxed in
the final couplet: "So wanton, light and false, my love, are you, / I am
most faithless when I most am true" (*CP,* 570).

Behind this poem are the same intentions regarding love—idealistic,
free, unpossessive—that were explained in *The Story of a Lover,* by
Hutchins Hapgood, which appeared anonymously in 1919:[16]

> I met men and women who, with the energy of poets and idealists,
> attempted to free themselves from that jealousy which is founded on physical
> possession. . . . They tried to rid themselves of all pain due to the physical
> infidelities of their lovers or mistresses!—believing that love is of the soul,
> and is pure and intense only when freed from the gross superstitions of the
> past. And one of the gross superstitions seemed to them the almost instinc-
> tive belief that a sexual episode or experience with any other except the
> beloved is of necessity a moral or spiritual infidelity. . . .
>
> They highly demanded that the love relation should be free and indepen-
> dent, that it should be one in which proud and individual equals commune
> and communicate, and give to each other rich gifts, but make no demands
> and accept no sacrifices, and claim no tangible possession in the personality
> of the other.

Behind what seemed to many to be merely flippant and cynical in-
dulgence, there lay the claim of devotion to the highest ideal, preferable
by far to externalities such as vows publicly uttered. The claim is set
forth most beautifully in "O, think not I am faithful to a vow!" with its
"certain weight of line rhythm,"[17] balancing of terms, and alliteration,
bold in the early lines and subtler in the sestet.

The bantering climax of the sonnets on the love game comes with "I
shall forget you presently, my dear," which accepts with utter realism
the biological impulses of lovers that lead them to inconstancy and
experiment. The voice of cynical experience colloquially belittles any
heroic pretenses:

> . . . nature has contrived
> To struggle on without a break thus far,—
> Whether or not we find what we are seeking
> Is idle, biologically speaking. (*CP*, 571)

Critics approved some poems of the volume: "Recuerdo" and "Macdougal Street," for example, though both have a touch of sentimentality. The former also has straight-forwardness, honest realistic details, and the excitement of young love, fresh and gay. The latter begins with a near-quotation of a ballad opening; but the lines in parentheses take the poem out of the ballad category and give it distinction as the speaker, lying awake late in the night, explains her feelings. She is (again) The Girl, feeling a love that is but reluctantly acknowledged and never publicly admitted.

In retrospect, the belittling of Millay on account of *A Few Figs from Thistles* seems foolish. Millay had wit. Should she be censured for using it, any more than should Suckling, Belloc, Swift, or Oliver Wendell Holmes for witty and satirical verses? *Figs* is a product of a "new woman" and of a gay and defiant satirist, merely one element in her personality, one facet of her versatility. Could any reader of the poet's next volume, *Second April,* believe that the publication of *Figs,* however naughty or meretricious some of the poems may have seemed, had in any way diminished the excellence of the new collection?

Second April

Second April is distinguished in several respects: it has considerable variety; it stresses the elegiac note and exhibits greater realism than the earlier volumes; its technical achievements are noteworthy; and it shows new metrical experiments. The second April represents a time of saddened, disillusioned maturity. Except for "Journey" (published in *Forum* [May 1913]) the poems were written during 1918–20, the poet's disenchanting New York years. "Journey" is notable for its observation of nature, Keatsian richness of detail, and the eloquent rhythm of the blank-verse lines toward the end with their heaped-up stresses.

The rapture that beauty gives, the shattering power of that rapture, and the poet's sadness that beauty must die are expressed in "The Death of Autumn," "Wild Swans," and "Assault." The last poem sets forth the idea most directly: "I am waylaid by Beauty. . . . / Oh, savage

Beauty, suffer me to pass . . ." (*CP,* 77). There is nothing in her heart, we are told in "Wild Swans," "Nothing to match the flight of wild birds flying." This eight-line poem with its irregular rhyme pattern closes with the plea: "Wild swans, come over the town, come over / The town again, trailing your legs and crying!" (*CP,* 124). A bold metrist made two separate feet of "wild swans" in the first of the two lines just quoted.

The worship of earthly beauty is also the theme of the "devious, supramundane allegory,"[18] "The Blue-Flag in the Bog" (*CP,* 55–65). The end of the world having come, through fire, God invites the victims to enjoy Heaven; but the narrator—a child—cannot bring herself to leave the familiar home until a sign comes. It is a beautiful blue-flag still unconsumed, which she protects like a little mother until the God of love and light rescues them and in consideration of human love for beauty agrees that "In some moist and Heavenly place / We will set it out to grow." The poem has obvious similarities to "Renascence"—the childish phrasing and point of view, the rapture over nature—but it has more homeliness. There is a Pre-Raphaelite air about it—an effect like that of the early poetry of D. G. Rossetti and Morris—produced by diction reminiscent of hymns and a Pre-Raphaelite exactitude of detail.

The poem is in trochaic tetrameter throughout, and many stanzas have a fine verse-movement. It shows also Millay's capability for striking metaphor—"fare you well, you shuddering day, / With your hands before your face!"—and for words used with surprising precision, as in "Not a glance brushed over me"; in "And the bottom of the sea / Was as brittle as a bowl"; and in the word *rotted* in stanza 27 (*CP,* 61).

The narrator can think of Heaven only as alien; the blue-flag is the symbol of those things that she truly *knew*; and paradoxically it provides Heaven with the only thing—one that can grow and develop—which can make the static perfection of Heaven, with its "windless hills," habitable by the earth-loving, earth-loyal human soul.

Allegorically, human desire can triumph; but *Second April* contains many poems of loss, sadness, or stark despair. Occasionally, homely details of everyday life are used with telling effect, as in "Alms" and "Lament." "Alms" is an extended metaphor: the heart is a house which the housekeeper tends numbly and mechanically through the winter: "I light the lamp and lay the cloth, / I blow the coals to blaze again; / But it is winter with your love, / The frost is thick upon the pane" (*CP*, 88). "Lament," as Padraic Colum pointed out, "has overpoweringly the sense of things that are handled."[19] A young widow facing an empty future voices her despair while trying to get up courage to raise her two children. The poem is in duple meter:

> Listen, children:
> Your father is dead.
> From his old coats
> I'll make you little jackets;
> I'll make you little trousers
> From his old pants.
> There'll be in his pockets
> Things he used to put there,
> Keys and pennies
> Covered with tobacco. . . .(*CP*, 103)

Though the manner is not Wordsworthian, here is a simplicity that Wordsworth would have approved: a situation from humble life in which "the essential passions of the heart" are poetically revealed.

Equivalent material of nature and landscape, most precisely observed and expressed, is found in "Elegy before Death." Housman and Teasdale may well be in Millay's mind, but the poem need fear no comparisons; of its kind, nothing can be finer. The poet-lover, who is envisioning the death of the beloved, projects her imagination into the future to perceive that situation, in which—although it seems unbelievable—earth's diurnal course will be unchanged and the world's work continue:

> There will be rose and rhododendron
>   When you are dead and underground;
> Still will be heard from white syringas
>   Heavy with bees, a sunny sound;
>
> Still will the tamaracks be raining
>   After the rain has ceased, and still
> Will there be robins in the stubble,
>   Grey sheep upon the warm green hill. (*CP*, 69)

Both the vowel music and the management of the consonants are superb here, the *o* in *rose* and *rhododendron,* the long *a*'s and *e*'s; the *d*'s and *s*'s in stanza one; the *st*'s, *t*'s, and *r*'s of stanza two. "Heavy" is exactly right, and "sunny sound" performs the same sort of poetic work as Keats's "beaker full of the warm South." The shaping, constructive personality of the dead man is suggested in stanzas three and four by the ugly or common things that will miss his handling them: the "sullen plough-land," "the may-weed and the pig-weed"—

> These, and perhaps a useless wagon
> Standing beside some tumbled shed.
>
> Oh, there will pass with your great passing
> Little of beauty not your own,—
> Only the light from common water,
> Only the grace from simple stone!

The beautiful music of "Song of a Second April" is somewhat more reminiscent of Housman, but all the material has been completely translated from Shropshire to New England. The disillusioned poet takes a little heart because, ". . . in this dourest, sorest / Age man's eye has looked upon," nature still creates beauty ("Doubt No More That Oberon," *CP*, 102).

She can assert, too, in "The Bean-Stalk," the pride of the creator of poetry, the "maker." Thus the greatness and the value of the imagination in such a harsh world are stressed. The poet, having "built" the bean-stalk into the sky, tells of the dangerous but exhilarating climb to such heights; earth seems gone, "the little dirty city" nothing but a "whirling guess." The sensations of climbing in a cold wind are excitingly expressed. Finally, the climber asserts (should one say God-like?) equality with the Giant who has created the sky:

> Your broad sky, Giant,
> Is the shelf of a cupboard;
> I make bean-stalks, I'm
> A builder, like yourself,
> But bean-stalks is my trade,
> I couldn't make a shelf,
> Don't know how they're made,
> Now, a bean-stalk is more pliant—
> La, what a climb! (*CP*, 73)

The vivaciousness and boyish brashness of this poem are remarkable. Millay freshened the meter by a device of irregularly spaced rhymes from one to six lines apart—a device she often used in later work.

A great contrast is seen in "Spring," which opens the volume and is her first venture into free verse. "Beauty is not enough," she announces. April always reveals the renewal of life: "It is apparent that there is no death." But

> Life in itself
> Is nothing,
> An empty cup, a flight of uncarpeted stairs.
> It is not enough that yearly, down this hill,
> April
> Comes like an idiot, babbling and strewing flowers. (*CP*, 53)

Against the preceding images, the final Ophelia-spring image makes April seem purposeless.

"Elaine" and "To a Poet That Died Young" show Millay's long-standing interest in Tennyson's work; the latter poem with its skillful allusions provides a tribute to the early Tennyson:

> Still, though none should hark again,
> Drones the blue-fly in the pane,
> Thickly crusts the blackest moss,
> Blows the rose its musk across,
> Floats the boat that is forgot
> None the less to Camelot. (*CP*, 91)

Second April also contains two poems of rather impressive length, "Ode to Silence" and "The Poet and His Book." Although Edmund Wilson said the "Ode" was one of the poems of Millay's New York period that most impressed him[20] and although it is composed with great technical skill (Cook called it "superbly musical, rivaling Tennyson"[21]), it has received little acclaim. Bynner called it "mouldy Elizabethan stuff."[22] Strictly speaking, it is not Elizabethan; it is an example of the free ode and reminds one of comparable things in the great ode tradition from Francis Thompson back to Milton.

Like "Exiled" and "Pastoral," the "Ode" comes out of dissatisfaction with New York. The poet searches for Silence, sister of the Muses,

whom she calls "Beauty veiled from men and Music in a swound." Her
shrines are noisy now; she is not to be found on earth or in Hell or in
Heaven. Finally, "compassionate Euterpe," the Muse of lyric poetry,
appropriately explains that Silence inhabits a province beyond Death or
Life, Heaven or Hell, the province of Oblivion; and the poet says she
will seek her there. The first three sections of the "Ode" are best; much
that follows is over-parenthetical and wordy. One can pick out various
fine passages, such as "And cymbals struck on high and strident faces /
Obstreperous in her praise / They neither love nor know . . ." (CP,
109). Some other notable lines are in the pastoral tradition, involving
flowers: "There twists the bitter-sweet, the white wisteria / Fastens its
fingers in the strangling wall, . . ." (CP, 114).

   Finest of all is the superbly satisfying "And will not Silence know /
In the black shade of what obsidian steep / Stiffens the white narcissus
numb with sleep?" (CP, 110). Maxwell Anderson was probably right,
however, in saying that the poem is "an artificial ecstasy; exquisite
treatment cannot save it."[23]

   "The Poet and His Book" (CP, 82–87)—not her book—is a plea for
survival through the continuing life of her poems. The work, in
trochaic meter, has an eight-line stanza with a nicely varied pattern of
line-length and rhyme and a mixing of "the sense of actual things" with
music, characteristic of seventeenth-century poetry, as Padraic Colum
observed.[24] This actuality of things is sharply conveyed in stanza five,
where the author thinks of the book

> Waiting to be sold
>   For a casual penny,
> In a little open case,
>   In a street unclean and cluttered,
>   Where a heavy mud is spattered
> From the passing drays. . . .

Her imaginative power shines in stanza seven, which combines scientific knowledge with the wittily macabre vision of the actual corpse.
Also her knowledge of people and her sympathy are revealed in the
catalogue of those to whom she appeals. She is especially sensitive to the
boys and girls whom she sees in some attic, "By a dripping rafter /
Under the discoloured eaves," lifting her book "out of trunks with
hingeless covers." To them she makes her final plea for remembrance:

> Flat upon your bellies
> By the webby window lie,
>   Where the little flies are crawling,
>   Read me, margin me with scrawling,
> Do not let me die!

The last stanza is a defiant assertion paralleling that of the first stanza: only the body can be brought to earth; but the spirit, the essential "I," will survive.

Millay's elegiac note is especially beautiful in her "Memorial to D. C.," the "perfect bits of tenderness"[25] in memory of Dorothy Coleman, a Vassar student who died in 1918. Part five, "Elegy," with its long stanzas in trochaic tetrameter and irregular rhyme-schemes, seems the finest of these "little elegies." In the background is the concept of the conservation of matter: the body will be transmuted into other forms—"will sweetly / Blossom in the air." But the voice will be lost. In stanza two the poet recalls with fine connotative force many sounds; and in stanza three she brings the poem to its restrained and perfect climax where assonance and alliteration are at their best:

> But the music of your talk
> Never shall the chemistry
> Of the secret earth restore.
> All your lovely words are spoken.
> Once the ivory box is broken,
> Beats the golden bird no more.[26] (*CP*, 123)

"Passer Mortuus Est" (*CP*, 75), with its touching allusion to Lesbia and her dead sparrow of Catullus's famous poem 3,[27] stresses the omnipotence of devouring death. The lyric is a triumph of diction. Vanished Rome is made vivid in stanza two by the precision of "sheer libation" equated with "old rain"; and "the little petulant hand" of Lesbia makes us feel both the reality and the pathos of vanished loves. Stanza three shows an honest modern girl's unconcern over her "erstwhile dear" (like Clodia's over Catullus); but though their love died, like the sparrow and like Lesbia herself, surely it was no less real for being transient—like Lesbia.[28]

"Weeds" (*CP*, 74) expresses the feelings of an outcast, a Cain-figure, glad to find a fitting refuge from hatred in a waste place among daisies and sorrel; "the brow accurst" is equated with the "damnèd seeds" of weeds. "Pastoral" uses rural material differently, contrasting constant city noise with pleasant, occasional country sounds—like "the soft shock / Of wizened apples falling . . ." (CP, 76). Exact diction economically reveals sharp details of remembered country life.

Second April also contains twelve sonnets; some—already noted— were inspired by Millay's love for Ficke. The first of the twelve, "We talk of taxes, and I call you friend," had been published in the Dial (28 December 1918) with the title "Quanti Dolci Pensier, Quanti Disio."[29] "Well enough we know," Millay says, how passion will overcome the lovers and "how such matters end." But sophistication will not lessen the greatness of the experience, joined in their passion by such heroines as Isolde, Guinevere, and Francesca (CP, 572).

Other sonnets (CP, 574, 577, 583) also make use of literary or classical allusion. But number 4 (CP, 575) is rather incongruously contemporary. Nine of the twelve are Petrarchan sonnets, with numbers 1, 2, 4, and 5 in the exacting four-rhyme form. Number 10 (CP, 581) inveighs in the Shakespearean vein against "unscrupulous Time." Thus the group possesses considerable variety.

Numbers 2, 3, and 11 are exceptionally good; but nearly every one of the sonnets has some weakness. In general, the sestets are more sucessful than the octaves. In number 8, for example, lines 2–3 have comparatively hackneyed phrases: "This flawless, vital hand, this perfect head, / This body of flame and steel . . . (CP, 579). Yet the sestet is simple, fresh, and affecting. Likewise, in sonnet 12, as Padraic Colum remarked, the octave is not immediately clear.[30] The sonnet seems to say, "Shall I put away this mouth of clay and these mortal bones for your sake, my lord? Shall I put away these mortal bones for the fever and sweat of human love?" But surely the sestet implies quite a different idea: "Shall I put away Pieria for your sake?" "This mouth" and "these mortal bones" are those of "my lord." They are not grammatically in apposition with "lord" but with "your so passing sake," taken to represent "lord." Such appositional looseness is to be found from time to time in Millay. She wrote with the copiousness of an Elizabethan; and her rich and copious flow occasionally betrayed her. Second April was, nevertheless, a considerable achievement, which put her, O. W. Firkins said, "among the vivid possibilities"[31] of becoming one of the great American poets of the twentieth century.

The Harp-Weaver and Other Poems

As in *Second April,* many of the poems in *The Harp-Weaver* are written in a mood of disillusionment, grief, or resignation; every spring must be followed by autumn, the slant-rhymed "Autumn Chant" reminds us (*CP,* 152), expressing with its pictorial, symbolic, and philosophical elements the theme of beauty rising from the dust to which it must return. Human life is assailed with hardship ("Scrub"), death ("Siege"), and misunderstanding ("Hyacinth"). Yet the "growing heart" needs fullness of experience for its mature satisfactions; so the poet finds reward in the "meagre shapes of earth," the bitterness of reality symbolized by "the smell of tansy" (*CP,* 151). She can appreciate beauty in unusual places and forms—difficult beauty—scorning conventional beauty, as in Sonnet 20 (*CP,* 603). Grief cannot destroy her response to beauty—thus "The Wood Road" is a converse of the bitter "Spring" in *Second April.* She distrusts ease and wealth which dull desire; if there is "no wine / So wonderful as thirst," it is best to have a hungry heart ("Feast," *CP,* 158). In poems praising deprivation or plainness ("The Dragonfly," "The Goose-Girl," *CP,* 162, 161), the author chooses "honest things," dull simplicity, the common lot of man. In spirit such poems are akin to "Renascence" although the tone is different: by moral effort one achieves a victory over the limitations of environment.

Many poems in the volume reveal the various responses of women in love; several of them—accomplished poems in ballad or folksong style—remind one of Housman or Hardy. "The Spring and the Fall" contrasts the romance of courtship with eventual rough familiarity, even cruelty, that "broke my heart in little ways" (*CP,* 168). In an excellent analysis Minot praises this poem for its skillful use of "repetition and variation on repetition," its "mastery of sound," and "intricate music."[32] A contrasting poem, "Keen," praises the early death of the lover: "Blessèd be Death, that cuts in marble / What would have sunk to dust!" (*CP,* 171). "The Pond" is a clear vignette in which the behavior of a girl-suicide is very plausibly sketched. Edward Davison praised it for its fine restraint.[33]

The poet's sincere, feminine personality speaks out realistically for women—for girls who have desires and experiences unsuspected by their elders, who are dismayed and disgusted by their cramped lives, or who insist on being independent. In various of these poems, The Girl[34] reveals an inner life that contrasts with outer appearances. In "Departure" she declares: "It's little I care what path I take" (*CP*, 163); then, concealing her feelings, she tells her mother that nothing ails her and she will make tea. This poem has the feel of a ballad and, with its simple vocabulary, stresses plain and ugly details, such as *rut, weedy rocks, dump, dock, ditch*. (It would, however, be better without the second stanza.) "Humoresque," compressed into two stanzas, ironically contrasts a girl's supposed innocence with her sordid experience of seduction and the murder of her lover. In a bitter soliloquy "The Betrothal," a girl reveals her cold decision to let herself be married to a man who wants her although—utterly without hope—she loves another.

Millay speaks frankly of bodily appetites, which women share with men; but she does not idealize them; she tends to scorn them. With cool disdain she separates blood from brain in Sonnet 18, acknowledging that a woman has certain needs and is subject to temptations which leave her "once again undone, possessed." But she ends with ironic contempt: "I find this frenzy insufficient reason / For conversation when we meet again" (*CP*, 601). Always she thinks in terms of a dichotomy between body and mind or soul.

Various *Harp-Weaver* sonnets celebrate love, generally with sadness or resignation, expecting it not to last. Such a one is "Pity me not" (*CP*, 589), a "fine example of a sonnet based on a single dominant image."[35] Yet Millay's idealism is not easily destroyed; she can become reconciled to change and loss, even death, as in Sonnet 9; but the "wound that will never heal" is "that a dream can die" (*CP*, 592). Maturity has brought bitterness and pain. In Sonnet 11 (*CP*, 594) she compares herself to a tree in autumn—"My sky is black with small birds bearing south"—and in Sonnet 19 to a lonely winter tree, its boughs silent, the birds gone. She can speak frankly of bygone loves; but she has only their ghosts to remember, and the memory brings pain: "I cannot say what loves have come and gone, / I only know that summer sang in me / A little while, that in me sings no more" (*CP*, 602).

Sonnets 13–16 deal with disease, despair, and death. Millay dictated Sonnet 13 to Ficke at Croton-on-Hudson when he was helping her during her convalescence in 1923. This funeral sonnet, a poem of deep despair, probably represents something of her hopeless feeling that summer. The misery of the sad "similar years" is finely expressed through the unifying details of the funeral image, and the poem ends with a death wish: "I would at times the funeral were done / And I abandoned on the ultimate hill" (*CP,* 596). Sonnets 14 and 15 are about people seriously ill. The first was published in *Vanity Fair* (June 1923) under the title "To a Dying Man." It is constructed in terms of a simile: "Your face is like a chamber where a king / Dies of his wounds. . . ." This complicated, somewhat confused poem is a tribute to the heroic demeanor of a person facing certain death; "you see," the reader is told, "fronting on your windows hopelessly, / Black in the noon, the broad estates of Death" (*CP,* 597). Sonnet 15 conveys how much the attentions of even a light-minded "Columbine" can mean to a man sick in the hospital. Sonnet 16 was published in *Ainslee's* (December 1918). It is composed of conceits depending on the classical concept of Hades.[36]

In spite of life's afflictions and sorrows, beauty abounds. The last three sonnets deal with beauty in different ways. Sonnet 20 (*CP,* 603) reminds one of the beauty to be found in fungus and mildew, in oil-filmed ditches, and in logs of scummy, frog-inhabited pools. The poet is disdainful of the "craven faces" too fastidious to endure unconventional, "difficult" beauty. This attitude fits in with her assertions of her greed for experience. The dynamic Sonnet 21 (*CP,* 604) has a picture of children playing, leaping, and running. The sestet asserts that death will still "these lovely tossing limbs"—but beauty and strength seem immortal.

The final sonnet, "Euclid alone has looked on Beauty bare" (*CP,* 605), with its magnificent first and last lines, has its matrix in a kind of Shelleyan Platonism, in an extreme Idealism. The utmost beauty, the pure concept uncontaminated with any physical representation, the perfect pattern that governs every physical manifestation of beauty, is honored in it. The poet who found mathematics her most difficult subject elected to praise conceptual beauty via the author of the *Elements,* Euclid, the famous geometer of whom it has been said: "He created a monument that is as marvelous in its symmetry, inner beauty, and clearness as the Parthenon, but incomparably more complex and more durable."[37] In a letter of 11 September 1920, Millay coupled Bach, "so pure, so relentless and incorruptible," with geometry and her "sonnet to Euclid."

In the octave of the sonnet the poet cites Euclid as the only one who could apprehend intellectual beauty, contrasting him with those who, being unable to free themselves from personal considerations, only

"prate of Beauty." The praters about Beauty—the "geese" that "gabble
and hiss"—are invited to keep silent, to "lay them prone upon the
earth," and to attempt contemplation of the "nothing, intricately
drawn nowhere" but in the mind. In the sestet the poet apostrophizes
that splendid moment, "O blinding hour, O holy, terrible day," when
Euclid first experienced the pure vision. In the last sentence she points
out that those who approximate such an experience—"once only and
then but far away"—are fortunate. The poem gains tension from the
paradox of a nothing drawn nowhere which can be observed; a nothing
in "shapes of shifting lineage" can be observed. One supposes that the
geometrical concepts are shapes with a shifting lineage because they can
be derived logically from whatever postulates the geometer begins
with.

In the contrast of geese and heroes (lines 6–7), she may have had in
mind Plato's myth of the cave in *The Republic.* If so, the geese are like
those prisoners underground, chained neck and leg in "dusty bondage," gabbling about glories and honors according to their false
notions. The hero (a Euclid) desires to see reality in the "luminous" air
of the upper world, which Plato called the world of knowledge. The one
who leaves Plato's cave is at first blinded by the sunlight: "O blinding
hour, . . ." The words *vision* and *light,* because of their connotations,
have both literal and metaphorical meaning. *Anatomized* seems a
strange word to apply to light. Light dissected?—analyzed? Perhaps it
is anatomized in the sense of mental light, conceptual knowledge,
divided into the particular geometrical elements of the theorems.

"Beauty bare" in the first line refers to the beauty of pure intellectual
concept; still, it is a personification; and in the twelfth line, divine
Beauty is to be seen as a goddess, like a Diana at her bath. Few human
beings have heroic encounters with divinities, especially unclothed
divinities. Thus the last sentence about the fortunate ones who have
heard from a distance the sound of the divinity's footsteps is relevant. So
great is the divine power that the time of such a direct encounter would
be marked as a "holy, terrible day"; and the power involved in the lesser
experience of hearing is suggested by "massive sandal" and "stone."

Millay set herself difficult problems in these sonnets; fifteen of them
are in the Petrarchan pattern, eight of these using only four rhymes.
Sentence units are usually few; Sonnet 1 contains only one sentence, and

the control of the material, since Millay is addicted to involved and parenthetical constructions, becomes a challenge. Sonnet 12 has an interesting flow of rhythm, seven lines being run-on; Sonnet 19 has six run-on lines; Sonnet 20 has seven. In contrast, Sonnet 8 has not a single run-on line; thus its colloquial tone is enhanced, and it becomes very sprightly. The skill with which the poet manipulates sounds in beautiful patterns of alliteration and assonance is remarkable, especially in sonnets 4, 6, 10, 18, 21, and 22.

The Harp-Weaver and Other Poems contains a few poems in free verse, none very impressive. "To One Who Might Have Borne a Message" speaks of a girl "Now two years dead, / Whom I shall always love." The message-bearer must tell her "That I love easily, and pass the time" (*CP*, 189). Millay may have been writing to John Reed, who died in 1920, about Dorothy Coleman, who died in 1918. Two pieces stand apart from the rest of the volume; these are the title-poem and the seventeen "Sonnets from an Ungrafted Tree." The volume was dedicated to Millay's mother, the inspiration of the title-poem.[38] "The Ballad of the Harp-Weaver" is a story of self-sacrifice by a poverty-stricken mother for her son. The child had no clothes, and all through the autumn the weather grew colder, the situation more desperate, with ". . . nothing in the house / But a loaf-end of rye, / And a harp with a woman's head / Nobody will buy" (*CP*, 177). The mother held her son in her lap, chafed his bones to warm him, and made him happy singing; but by the night before Christmas their state was critical. In the night the mother rose and on the strings of the harp wove "wonderful things," magical garments fit for a king's son. In the morning the boy found his mother at the harp,

> And her hands in the harp-strings
>   Frozen dead.
> And piled up beside her
>   And toppling to the skies,
> Were the clothes of a king's son,
>   Just my size. (*CP*, 183–84)

Allegorically implied here are all the sacrifices of Mrs. Millay, who enabled her brilliant daughter to have royal gifts though the family was poor—the beautiful, romantic "garments" of music, poetry, ideas—

the clothing of mind and heart, for which the daughter remained ever grateful.

The poem is a skillful mixture of ballad and nursery rhyme. Well organized, its thirty stanzas are divided evenly at the night-before-Christmas point; it uses six stanzas with an extra line to achieve variety and to indicate organization.

In "Sonnets from an Ungrafted Tree" (*CP*, 606–22) Millay relates the experience of "the New England woman" who returns in winter to her dying husband's house to care for him although she has no love for him. The stark directness and the physical and psychological realism of the sequence are notable. The same observation of details that one finds, for example, in "Souvenir"—". . . naked blackberry hoops / Dim with purple chalk" (*CP*, 159)—appears in these sonnets with utmost vividness; the startling precision of the imagery, both visual and auditory, is impressive. Besides the immediate experience of the woman "ungrafted," Millay reveals, directly and symbolically, something of the woman's character and her past. As a young woman in that house, she had been blithe; she had wanted beauty and had painted a butter-tub and planted red geraniums in it. Now their stalks are rotted, and she cannot imagine a time, even in summer, when constant rain will not beat down upon the house. She had been betrayed by loneliness and desire into marriage with a commonplace fellow "not her spirit's mate."

At the end of Sonnet 10 the "oak tree's shadow . . . deep and black and secret as a well" is an ominous symbol. Her impatience and lack of judgment have already been implied in Sonnet 3, in which she picks up wood in the woodshed, "selecting hastily small sticks of birch, / . . . that instantly will leap / Into a blaze," and does not think ahead to a day when only big green logs and "knotty chunks" will remain— "(That day when dust is on the wood-box floor, / And some old catalogue, and a brown, shriveled apple core)" (*CP*, 608). As she blows upon the "stubborn coal," she is "mindful of like passion hurled in vain / Upon a similar task, in other days . . ." (Sonnet 4). When the husband failed to respond to her love, her life became an exercise in frustration, suppressed desires, and hardening resentment, and she turned into a sour, knurly apple.

During this nightmare interval (Sonnet 13) she finds some consolation in homely routine details of farmhouse work and in cleaning up the neglected place. Millay's abundant and accurate knowledge of such details of country life will instantly be vouched for by anyone who knows it. The ordeal ends at last with the death of the husband, and she finally sees him as an unfamiliar person. The work ends with this memorable simile:

> She was as one who enters, sly, and proud,
> To where her husband speaks before a crowd,
> And sees a man she never saw before—
> The man who eats his victuals at her side,
> Small, and absurd, and hers: for once, not hers, unclassified. (*CP,* 622)

In their rhythms and concrete details these sonnets are close to the honest, direct poetry of the early William Morris; and their spirit is implied in Tennyson's "Mariana," which Millay admired. As a sonnet sequence the work is related to Meredith's *Modern Love* and Ficke's *Sonnets of a Portrait Painter*—which are in the background of other Millay sonnets, too.[39] Meredith used a sixteen-line "sonnet" in *Modern Love*; similarly, Millay took liberties with the sonnet form in "Sonnets from an Ungrafted Tree." She used three quatrains and a couplet, but the third quatrain rhymes *e f f e,* and the fourteenth line has seven feet. The usual Shakespearean content-divisions are ignored in most of the sonnets, which are treated as stanzas, fourteeners.

Chapter Three

"Beautifully Written, after a Flippant Fashion"

Millay's prose mainly comprises her short stories, under her own name and under her pseudonym Nancy Boyd, and satiric writings collected in *Distressing Dialogues*. She also wrote a prose play, the article "Fear," a preface to translations from, and a "Biographical note" about, Baudelaire.

Her "Nancy Boyd" stories published in *Ainslee's* between 1919 and 1921 are all stories of courtship which involve physical and temperamental attraction and often love. In them three themes are paramount: the question of love versus career, the approval of Greenwich Village attitudes, and the overwhelming of men by love.

As we know, the problem of love versus career was of great importance to Millay in her Greenwich Village days and may have presented itself earlier.[1] In "Young Love" (*Ainslee's,* May 1919), the heroine,[2] although mightily attracted to an uncultured young man, is happy when, through accident, he leaves and her musical career is preserved. Millay takes up another phase of physical and temperamental attraction in "Nothing in Common" (September 1920). A bright young woman who is a professional painter is impressed by a culturally illiterate but handsome and innocently romantic young man. Their hostess at a house party insists that they have nothing in common; but when the heroine, an experienced person rather like one of the Village girls, decides she is truly in love, nothing else matters. The issue of her independence and her painting career is not raised. The respect given here to mad youth, beauty, and reckless gaiety is in keeping with some of Millay's sonnets.

Of all these stories "The White Peacock" is the most revealing. It involves a beautiful "hybrid," a girl of Chinese-Japanese-French blood with whom an American is in love. Antoinette had lived in the Orient, but her father had put her in a Quaker school in the United States.

Because, as she explains, he "feared always for my so strange soul if I should continue . . . a worshiper of idols, he bade me forswear forever great Buddha, and Shaka, and my holy ancestors, and even his own Sainte Vierge Marie and Jesus Christ, her son, and my Sainte Antoine de Padoue, and to love God simply, simply. . . ." She particularly remembers a bird at the palace in Canton: ". . . there was one white, white . . . *peacock,* in the courtyard, that I feared, and ran from, and loved, and followed. He died." Bailey, the American, declaring his love, belittles her interest in "these candles and gods and crucifixes and—and *spells*. . . !" (*Ainslee's,* January 1920, p. 100).

Against her cheek she presses a little fan of white peacock feathers: "into her eyes again . . . came that strange look of passionate surrender to something he did not see" (101). They struggle over the fan; presently she is prostrate before an embroidery of a white peacock on the wall: "on a black ground shot with threads of gold, a white peacock, with a sensuous, languid body, and a cruel head, on which sat like a crown a fan-shaped jewelled aigrette, and from which winked a slanting, ruby eye" (101–2). She prays to the peacock image:

Ah, toi que j'adore! . . . Is it that you are mine, or not, in this moment, my terrible and proud? See, I touch you—you do not scream at me; I lay my hand on your body, you do not tear my flesh! It is because you are dead! Dead! Yes, yes, my dear one, that is it! I fear you no longer, no! See what I dare to do! Ah, but I hate you . . . so much, my adored one. I stroke you, I ruffle your soft side, I kiss your cold, red eye![3] (102).

Bailey feels "a surging and blinding jealousy of the thing, this bird, this presence, whatever it was, which she loved more than she loved him." Finding the girl in a trance, he rips the embroidery down and burns it in the fireplace, along with her fan. He bears her to the bed while the peacock burns. "As the room grew darker under the expiring flame, she ceased struggling . . ." (102).

Although she tells him in the morning that she loves him, he finds her at night praying to St. Anthony of Padua (invoked to find lost articles) to give her back her peacock. She orders Bailey to depart:

I pity thee and I wish thee good fortune. But I do not love thee! I tell thee this at once, in cruelty, for I pity thee, and would have thee find for thyself soon a lovely lady with yellow hair, that is but one lady always, and does not change at all! (103)

He is aghast—"But, 'Toinette, after last night, dearest, you can't mean that—" She replies: "Last night—pouf! what was it? A man and woman in each other's arms! Sweet, yes, perhaps you call ecstasy, but, la! not rare! As for me—ah. I slept after a little, and dreamed, and it was not of thee" (104). He cannot understand such a dismissal. He asks—since the peacock is gone—if there is anything standing between them. Then he finds that she is holding a brass bowl, which contains—"the ashes of the white peacock" (104).

This symbolic story is psychologically among the most interesting of Millay's writings. The Oriental background reflects her Oriental interests of 1919–20 and her acting in *The String of the Samisen*. More significantly, the heroine expresses the idea that the actions of the body, even the sexual congress, are of little importance—a doctrine clearly stated in Millay's sonnet "I, being born a woman and distressed" (*Complete Poems*, 601) and implied in some sonnets of *A Few Figs from Thistles*. For the heroine, as for Millay, what does count is something mystical, the white peacock; and the peacock symbolizes art, which for Millay is the art of poetry. The heroine's father saw that she had a "strange soul" and wanted her not to be a worshiper of idols; he bade her forsake her "holy ancestors" and placed her in a Quaker school, which would represent a practical simplicity at the utmost extreme from the exotic Orientalism of her temperament. The holy ancestors of Millay would be the great poets of the past. The "spell," in which the lover finds the heroine, suggests the ecstasy of poetic inspiration, during which a poet has no interest in ordinary matters, even lovers.

The heroine's attitude toward the peacock, like an artist's toward the demands of his art, is ambivalent: the bird with the cruel head and cold eye is something that she "feared, and ran from, and loved, and followed." It is a god, "terrible and proud" and capable of punishing its devotee, who, however, being separated from it, can only pray for reunion with it.

Here once more is a projection of Millay's struggle between love and career; the story shows clearly her conviction that nothing should be allowed a place in her life ahead of her poetry,[4] which is her religion. "The White Peacock" has the same theme as "Young Love"; but here the denouement comes about by no accident. The inspired woman, though she can be briefly overcome by the "poor treason" of the blood, is nevertheless dominant: she knows herself and understands how she reveres the "something beyond" more than she can love the simple young man. Even the ashes of the peacock-image are her greatest treasure. She is made Oriental to contrast both with the simple Bailey and with the usual Western woman who is "one lady always, and does not change at all!" The usual woman would be an ordinary practical person who is all woman, not woman and poet. The symbolic theme of "The White Peacock" parallels that of Millay's sonnet "Cherish you then the hope I shall forget." The fanatical devotion of the heroine to the peacock is that of Millay to Pieria, the realm of art for which she proudly renounces "the puny fever and frail sweat / Of human love . . ." (*Complete Poems*, 583).

"The Door" has for its setting a town on Penobscot Bay, where a woman novelist and an artist are vacationing. Her feminism causes a little friction, but they fall in love; and, trying to do something scandalous that will make people avoid them, they get the door open between their adjoining hotel rooms. Ironically, they receive even more attention from the other guests. They leave the hotel together, going, the author surmises

Heaven knows where—to one of those God-forsaken islands, I suppose, where you get sand in your stockings and salt in your hair and rheumatism in the calves of your legs, and go in swimming four times as often as you want to, just because you don't have to wear your Annette. And whether or not, before their departure, they had the good taste to drop in upon some languid justice of the peace and secure unto their radiant union his perfectly unimportant blessing, I cannot tell you. (*Ainslee's*, July 1919, p. 141)

Cynthia, the heroine, wears no wedding ring, it appears, nor does she go by the name of Mrs. Holloway—"but then she wouldn't anyway. These advanced thinkers are the devil and all to keep track of. Besides, as for myself, I never even wanted to know." The author did want to know what happened during their last three days at the hotel: was the door "kept piously closed—or honestly open—or sweetly and improperly ajar?" Cynthia would not tell.

This story smacks of Greenwich Village and achieves what readers came to recognize as the "Nancy Boyd" manner, a combination of wit and archness, high-falutin circumlocution, and a languid air of sophistication. The heroine feels the same overwhelming intensity of love that is expressed in many Millay sonnets. The story reflects Millay's disrespect for convention, her approval of nude bathing,[5] and her indignation toward those who interfere with a writer's work.

"The Dark Horse" (*Ainslee's,* September 1919) contrasts a wife who is an unworthy person—lazy, lying, faithless, and unappreciative of her husband—with the protagonist, a sensitive and emotional girl much like Millay, criticial of insincerity and artificiality and very responsive to beauty and its transience. Though the wife acknowledges that she has a model husband, her attitude is that expressed in some of the poems of *A Few Figs from Thistles*: "What I want is a faithless lover, a liar, a thief, a man it is impossible to trust. I pine for uncertainties. John is so constant, I have grown to look upon him as a piece of furniture!" (57). The protagonist, however, meditates upon John's face, "tragically sensitive, restless, inscrutable . . ." (58). Although unhappy over a seemingly hopeless love, the protagonist finally elopes with her lover—who is revealed as her unappreciative friend's husband. After the friend has so forthrightly wished her husband to be unfaithful, one can only feel that she has her comeuppance.

The protagonist's sorrows, her sensitivity, and her childlike sincerity in the midst of debasing sophistication insure the reader's sympathy. "Beloved child," John calls her. The term *child* becomes typical for the heroine of the Nancy Boyd stories.

In the fall of 1919 Millay informed Arthur Davison Ficke that she was writing under the name of Nancy Boyd. "Some of my stories," she said, "are good, some are bad,—almost invariably they are beautifully written, after a flippant fashion." Yet her next story, "The Seventh Stair" (*Ainslee's,* October 1919), a fifty-six page novelette, is poorer than the other stories. It contains a good deal of trite melodrama, lacks wit, and shows signs of hasty composition.[6] The style has little distinction. The story involves motifs of flight, wronged innocence, and social criticism as well as love and self-sacrifice. The plot is an involved one depending upon a series of revelations reluctantly brought forth. Much of the action takes place in Greenwich Village, especially in Charlton Street, where Millay had lived in 1918.

The story reflects Millay's interest in feminism, radical movements, and Oriental things. The sister of the hero engages in suffragist activities and labor agitation. Her trial (for the second time, with a hung jury) is parallel to the second *Masses* trial, which began on 1 October 1918 and which Millay attended. The hero has been to Japan and has Oriental decoration and clothing in his house. Millay acted in Rita Wellman's *The String of the Samisen* at the Provincetown Playhouse in January 1919. In 1920 she decorated her room in West 12th Street in Chinese style and wrote to Witter Bynner that she loved kimonos.

A spirit of rebellion against conventions and materialism is put in a favorable light. The rebellious heroine favors that which is real, sincere, honest, unaffected; her attitude is like that of the protagonist of "The Dark Horse"; and she is admired for courage and lack of sentimentality. Along with this spirit of rebellion is a Bohemian approval of spontaneity. The heroine impulsively went away with a stranger but refused to marry him—in the name of being "honest and real" (5). It is asserted that love is a rare thing but that those who love have all that matters, a doctrine asserted in later poems of Millay. The men in the story are overcome by love; they become women's adorers and whimpering slaves, abjectly grateful for the least tenderness. Such an attitude is in keeping with the doctrine of women's equality if not dominance in sexual matters, which was regarded as a fresh note in Millay's poetry.

"Innocents at Large" (*Ainslee's,* December 1919) is a slight story which emphasizes the importance of the real in contrast to the artificial and takes a tiny step in the direction of feminism: women characters are honored for being able to do something besides being decorative.

"Mr. Dallas Larabee, Sinner" was the last Nancy Boyd story to be published in *Ainslee's* (October 1920).[7] Its heroine desires freedom from conventional bonds, which she hopes to attain by being unconventional and even improper. Dallas Larabee, the sophisticate, is so affected by her innocence that he proposes to her, warning her that people who marry do not always remain married and asking her if she knows about "an institution no less divine than that of matrimony itself, namely the healing dispensation of divorce" (88). He says he is terrified of her, and when she casually lays her hand on his shoulder, he turns to her "with a little cry like a sob. . . ," saying, "My beautiful love! What have you done to me, Keane?" She confesses her love, he kisses her with "harsh kisses" (89), and the story ends thus with the snake driven from Eden and Larabee no sinner but a man of honor and tender sentiment toward his "foolish child."

Keane represents rebellious youth; but again the heroine is called *child* by her lover, the tender, strong protector—who, overcome by love, is turned into a terrified suppliant. The favorable view of divorce (humorously introduced even during the proposal) adds a touch of sophistication.

The last Nancy Boyd story was "Sentimental Solon" (*Metropolitan*, October 1921), a work on which Millay collaborated with her sister Norma and which she finished in Paris in the summer of 1921.[8] This is a gay, fantastic tale in which the Millay sisters' bent for satire and fun was given considerable latitude; it is a sort of spoof of trite literary situations, a fantasia of desire so imposed upon a realistic setting that for a good while the reader feels that it may turn out to be a dream. It is a kind of modern fairy tale—self-consciously done—that might have been written by a more literary O. Henry. The story is contrived to turn on the coincidental meeting of a pair of young authors and the revelation that both have a sense of honor and obligation as well as a sense of fun and a knowledge of *Alice in Wonderland*. Since each makes a sacrifice for the other, it reminds one of "The Gift of the Magi."

Both characters are described in terms of literary stereotypes. The girl is the Wonderful Person, Princess, Queen, Beautiful Fisher Maiden, Proud Beauty, Simple Country Girl, Heroine of the Story, Adventuress, Sultan's Favorite, Fascinating Widow, Woman-Who-Just-*Loved*-Boys, Rose of the Rancho. Solon the hero is by turns Page, Astrologer, Lord of the Manor, Tired Business Man, Villain, Man of Mystery, Man-with-the-Mustachios, Her Captor, Boy-She-Had-Known-from-Childhood, Bored Young Dog. Each of these designations indicates the mood in which the character speaks, or the role that he or she momentarily puts on.

The dialogue is a queer mixture of the kind of intimate illiteracy close friends or members of a family might use and the clichés of romance. Solon thinks of the heroine as a "cunnin' li'l thing"; in fact, he says "cunnin' li'l thing" to her "in a deep voice"! The overcute dialogue makes one believe that the story should be regarded chiefly as a spoof. This parody fairy tale of the metropolis points the way toward the fabulistic prose rehandlings of traditional material that Millay was to publish in *Vanity Fair* under her own name.

Millay's nine Nancy Boyd stories are fairly competent examples of the art of the short story. None of them is great; all of them are tailored to the patterns of the popular fiction magazine. They concern mainly writers and artists, people of the sort Millay knew, and Millay sensibly used settings that she was familiar with. She broke no new ground so far as technique is concerned, but the stories are above the average for potboilers. Several of them have a "Nancy Boyd" distinctiveness of style and tone as well as of character—chiefly the talented, independent woman at the end of World War I, much like Millay herself in spirit.

It must be Millay's own desire for independence, her own sympathy for feminism, that appear in these stories; yet, ironically, she also shows her own yearning for protection, if not domesticity. This yearning, taken one romantic step further, produces the hero who becomes the grateful slave of his beloved; the woman is thus able to remain dominant even in her surrender.[9]

Under her own name Millay published several stories in *Vanity Fair* during 1922 and 1923. They are quite different in intention and tone from her stories in *Ainslee's,* for they are fabulistic, fantastic, or fairy-tale–like pieces with satirical elements. "The Barrel" (July 1922) is a kind of moral apologue about Diogenes, who finds one night that a woman has moved into his barrel. He criticizes her and thinks that Man should do without women, but she insists that she has as much right to be there as he, and she is going to stay. She improves the place with a geranium and a mat saying PLEASE WIPE YOUR FEET; wanting to make him happy, she tells him that she has found an honest man. Still not happy, having quit his search and put out his lantern, he suddenly becomes old. She tells him that she doubts the man she found is really honest, and as Diogenes starts out again—though she had told him he was a fool to light the lantern each morning—"she stooped, and lighted it, and put it in his hand" (36).

Another tale that throws light on the masculine and the feminine and is much closer to Millay's own concerns is "The Key," a retelling of the story of Bluebeard and his seventh wife in pseudoarchaic style, rather like that of James Branch Cabell. Bluebeard leaves the key to a secret room with Yolaine and orders her not to open it. She customarily sits, pen in hand, before a folio of white paper but writes nothing. After four days he returns and asks for the key. She cannot tell him where it is. Finally it drops from her hair, and he knows that she has not entered the chamber, for no blood is on it. "But Bluebeard was sore amazed . . . , and the mind of his wife became a secret thing to him." She tells him she had only been thinking. Then he "felt that he must know her thought, or he could not live." He asked her what she had written. "Nothing." "But when he reached for the paper . . . , she caught it to her breast" and would have fled. "Whereat he . . . cried, 'If indeed it be nothing, wherefore would you shield it from me?'" "She answered . . . , 'I know not.'" When he demanded it, she "looked into his face, and answered, 'Never.'" Then he "laid hands upon his wife and slew her"; but when he looked at the paper, "it was innocent of writing" (94).

This new twist on the old story illustrates women's resistance to automatic male domination and Millay's resentment of any invasion of her privacy, such as she felt against Dell.

"The Platter" (March 1923) is an extension of a Mother Goose rhyme in which Jack Spratt tries to teach his overfat wife a lesson by buying a lean "embittered bachelor gander," which she refuses to cook. Jack leaves her to be an apprentice to a chemist's widow who is thin, tart-tongued, overtalkative, and too neat. After some months he returns to his wife, ready to admire her girth and to agree that both fat and lean should be eaten.

Another piece with marriage as its target is "The Woman Who Would Be Moving the Beds About," subtitled "A Little Homily for Housewives . . ." (February 1923). Every few weeks Mrs. Merris changes the places of the beds in the bedroom, to the exasperation of her husband, who, on coming home from his office finds not only the room but himself, unsettled. "Apart from this foible . . . she was a pearl among women. She was beautiful, intelligent, chaste, and had money in her own right." After four years he issues an ultimatum: promise never to move furniture, or he will leave. She keeps the promise six months but becomes thin and nervous, and a month later she leaves him. He tracks her all over the world and brings her back. With her mind on the stimulating things seen during her travels, she is no longer interested in moving beds. Evidently the story is a jibe at the stifling home life of the upper-class housewife with too little to do.

Both "Drama for the Deaf" and "'Say Shibboleth'—A Dialogue between a Sentimental Citizen and an Advertising Expert" (January, April 1923) are satires on stereotypes. In "Drama" Millay satirizes stereotyped dramatic situations and characters. A man bothered by a deaf wife who insists on going to the theater arranges for stereotyped plays with no speaking. She has no trouble with dialogue, and the action is perfectly clear in this "Drama for the Deaf"—which is so popular that all other theaters soon close. The tale, then, is really satire directed against silent movies.

In "'Say Shibboleth'" a citizen avers that America has no culture, it is impossible to make the American public think for itself, and he is worried about the country. The Advertising Expert says the result can easily be obtained by advertising: tell the public what to think, and that's what it thinks. Many "Useful Phrases" are not reasonable, but people believe them—Women and Children First, Survival of the Fittest, Food Will Win the War. People were fooled by "Freedom to Worship God"—freedom must always be *from*. Though thinking is painful, people could be made to think by using such phrases as Use Your Own Head—Accept No Substitutes often enough and in large enough letters. But a campaign would be costly; and "it will be impossible to find a man with money, who will be interested in having the public think for itself" (40).

These satirical efforts as well as the twenty-two "Nancy Boyd" pieces written by Millay in Europe, published in *Vanity Fair,* and collected in *Distressing Dialogues* (1924) fall into the category of Menippean satire. The volume includes nine little plays, or skits, usually with two characters, and other satires, essays, or fictions of some sort. Among the skits, "Here Comes the Bride" exposes family irritations aroused by arranging a fashionable wedding; "Tea for the Muse" brings out the inanities of conversation at a tea to which a poet has been invited but ignored; "For Winter, for Summer" reveals the female wiles that a wife uses to make her husband jealous and thus get permission to go on a hunting trip with him. "Honor Bright" is a slight story; "The Greek Dance" is a deadpan satiric essay, and "Look Me Up," a satiric essay gibing at American clubbiness and favoring privacy. "Art and How to Fake It" by means of letters of inquiry about art and Greenwich Village, with Nancy Boyd's replies, pokes fun at current fads; "Cordially Yours" provides forthright models for people who need "Our New Impolite Letter-Writer"; "Our All-American Almanac and Prophetic Messenger" consists of predictions from 1925 to 1953, all emphasizing triumphs of "Puritanism," such as 1 April, Anthony Comstock "proclaimed patron saint of America, 1926"; 13 July, "Card-playing abolished, 1925. Theatres closed, 1941."

Menippean satire "deals less with people as such than with mental attitudes";[10] in the typical pattern "the attack is managed under cover of a fable."[11] Because of these qualities Millay's satire has affiliations with the philosophical novel of Peacock and Cabell. Her Nancy Boyd *persona* is that of a modern, sophisticated, and emancipated young woman with responses generally contrary to those of the majority. John J. Patton emphasizes the irony and "relatively sustained and unremitting satire" of Millay's *Dialogues,* and indicates that their humor bears some resemblance to that of Robert Benchley and Stephen Leacock[12] (who were also writing for *Vanity Fair*). Perhaps Millay caught something of her ironic, mock-heroic style from Dorothy Parker, who wrote in a flippant, mock-heroic way in her 1918–19 reviews of plays for *Vanity Fair.*

Millay also wrote "The Murder in the Fishing Cat" (*Restaurant du Chat Qui Pêche*).[13] After the wife of a Paris restaurant owner runs off with a taxi driver and his business becomes very slow, the lonely proprietor gets in the habit of talking to an eel in his tank. When a customer orders eel, he reluctantly beats the eel to death, thinking of it as the taxi driver. Then he has fantasies, fears he has drowned his wife, and, deranged, buries the eel's remains in the garden. So this is not a murder story, not a mystery or detective story, but a psychological story after the fashion of Poe.[14] It is unlike her other fictions.

Some of Millay's satires are bounded by the early 1920s, but others, especially the fabulistic pieces, are psychologically penetrating and are concerned with human problems and relationships of timeless interest. Although done with the left hand,[15] Millay's prose writings of 1919–22, divided about equally between romance and satire, reveal her cleverness in adapting material to the demands of the magazines where she published, and, within the limits of those demands, a considerable range and effectiveness.

Chapter Four

"Bean-Stalks Is My Trade"

Writing drama appealed to Millay. She completed six plays, three in a play-writing course at Vassar, two on commission, and one—her most experimental achievement, the famous *Aria da Capo*—for the Play-wrights' Theatre. Even the Vassar apprentice work is written with considerable skill. In most of the plays the themes of honor and integrity predominate, along with romantic ideals of love and friendship.

The Princess Marries the Page

The Princess Marries the Page, her earliest attempt at play-writing, she had begun several years before taking the course.[1] A romantic work, the play has professional, realistic stage directions; but its atmosphere is child-like, that of fairy tale. As the play opens, ". . . in a very big chair, reading a very big book, sits the most beautiful Princess you have ever seen" (1). During her spirited conversation with a Page who sits on the window ledge, it is obvious that they are attracted to each other. The plot of the play is one of pursuit and protection. To find and capture the Page, there come in turn the Chancellor, the guard, and the King himself. While the Page hides in the ivy outside the tower, the Princess tells the Chancellor that he has not been *in* the tower. She faces a harder test with the soldiers, for she has learned that the Page is the son of the neighboring "Sullen King" and is presumably a spy. But she deceives the guard and manages temporarily to confuse her father with scoldings and accusations. When put to the ultimate test, she temporizes, lies, and is about to swear on her soul that she has not seen the Page—when he leaps into the room to save her soul. She tells her father that she will not live without the Page; if he is put to death, she will take her life. The evidence against the Page—a Prince, of course, and actually a King, for his father has just died—is cleared up; and he explains to the Princess that he has loved her since she was a child. The play has its fairy-tale ending, though without any embracing and love-making at

the close, quite properly, for the play was first acted by girls. In terms of
drama the poet achieves an excellent theatrical effect when the Page
leaps in crying "Lied—to shelter such a man" (39). The characters,
however, are chiefly conventional; the Princess, the sole female figure,
is a sprightly contrast to the others.

The play is in blank verse, with a good proportion of run-on lines.
Yet it has a mixture of styles; the author has not attained a firm dramatic
voice of her own. An early passage, set off from the main body of the
verse and supposed to be from a book the Princess is reading, sounds
Tennysonian or Pre-Raphaelite: "So then the maiden came / Clothed all
in delicate colours, like a garden, / And very sweet to smell . . ." (3).
Other passages have a romantic air mainly caught from *A Midsummer
Night's Dream,* and there are numerous other Shakespearean reminis-
cences such as the King's warning to his daughter (34–35). The tone of
later Elizabethan drama, especially that of John Webster, is heard in the
Princess's comments on dying (44). In contrast to the Elizabethan and
other romantic echoes, the Princess speaks at times in a colloquial
manner. Despite its youthful stylistic unsureness, the play is, as the
author herself decided years later, "rather pretty."[2]

Two Slatterns and a King

Two Slatterns and a King, the second Vassar play, which Millay called
a "Moral Interlude," is a merry, unabashed imitation of a Renaissance
interlude written in four-beat couplets. It has something of the tone of
John Heywood's interludes as well as the fluency of Chaucer.[3] Chance,
the "cunning infidel" (*Three Plays,* 3) who manages the action, is more
like Puck of *A Midsummer Night's Dream* than the Vice of a morality
play. The point of the little play (scarcely a dozen pages long) is that,
through effects of Chance, even a King may be made a laughingstock.

The King suddenly decides to marry. For his bride he wishes "that
maid whose kitchen's neatest," and he goes about inspecting kitchens.
Influenced by appearances while making his fairy-tale tests, he rejects
Tidy, usually a model of neatness, and marries Slut—to his regret. In
the mockery of "a King / Though a sublime and awful thing," (*Three
Plays,* 3) one senses an anti-authoritarian joy.

The Wall of Dominoes

The third Vassar play, *The Wall of Dominoes,* is a prose work with contemporary setting and characters. The action occurs in "a sitting-room in a New York house, artistically and somewhat excitingly furnished . . ."—a smart, up-to-date setting for a play dealing with topics of much concern to the college generation of 1917.[4] One sees that sophistication is attractive—but to what lengths should it be carried, and at what price procured?

The sophisticated protagonist—"a tall and beautiful girl of twenty-four"—explains to a friend that she was in love with a man but told herself that her feeling was just passion and lost him. "After that I didn't much care what I did—most anything to warm me up. I made up my mind . . . that . . . everything I really wanted to do, I would do—and that's what I've been doing ever since." She adds, however: "There were some things I just didn't want to do—without love. . . ."

She analyzes her situation in terms of the wall of dominoes, which gives the play its title. She had smoked alone, then in her room with others, "and then in public places, and if you smoke it's foolish to say that you don't drink, and if you drink a little, it looks as if you were scared to drink a lot. . . ." So she was surrounded, she says, by a wall of dominoes—"and the wind blew! and each one as it fell knocked down the next. . . . A few of my dominoes are still left standing . . . , but soon the wind will blow again,—and when the next one falls there will be nothing between me and destruction." One thing she would never do—wear hats with feathers; this "never" is another of the dominoes of her wall.

The action comes rapidly to its climax. A guest arrives—a married artist who is the man she loved. She invites him to take her out that evening. On returning, he says that he will not take her unless she loves him, but she is reluctant. The man gets her a hat because of the cold. Though the hat has a bird on it, she starts, laughing, to put it on. He is unconvinced that she loves him. Looking at the hat, she wishes she were dead—"I don't love anybody." He leaves, she weeps; then she says, "I guess I'd better put that hat back where it came from."

The play shows the author's interest in "daring" subjects: the dangers in living for the moment, doing merely as one pleases, and removing all restraints. Characteristic of the time, it focuses on the problems of a bachelor girl in New York. Patton relates the play, in manner, to *Good Gracious, Annabelle,* by Clair Kummer, a Broadway success of 1916. As he says, however, it is more than a farce; the heroine's bittersweet victory, her decision to keep to her code of honor by telling the truth at the cost of temporary thrills and of being thought stodgy, is a matter of excruciating strain. As in *The Princess Marries the Page,* honor and integrity are most significant values.

Unlike Millay's verse plays, this one-acter was never staged. Its realism and its treatment of contemporary manners—light and satirical in the early part—look forward to the Nancy Boyd stories and dialogues, and ultimately to *Conversation at Midnight.*[5]

Aria da Capo

Aria da Capo has the concern with mankind that one expects of a morality play. It begins as a harlequinade; the traditional figures of Pierrot and Columbine are sitting at opposite ends of a long table "with a gay black and white cloth, on which is spread a banquet." The table occupies the center of a set with "a merry black and white interior." The two diners seem a frivolous modern pair; yet Columbine is not so frivolous and changeable-fantastic as Pierrot. A literal-minded girl, she offsets his antics: she knows what day of the week it is; she thinks he drinks too much; she hopes that he loves her now and truly. Their conversation—Pierrot always taking the lead—comprises a few satirical comments on extremist movements of the day. Pierrot imagines himself a radical painter splashing on his canvas ". . . six orange bull's-eyes, four green pinwheels, / And one magenta jelly-roll,—the title / As follows: *Woman Taking in Cheese from Fire-Escape"* (*Three Plays,* 19). Then he becomes a pianist imaging Columbine in sound "on a new scale . . . / Without tonality. . . ." The title will be *Uptown Express at Six o'Clock.* Then he repels her, having become a socialist: "I love / Humanity; but I hate people" (20). These facile wisecracks are followed by equally unimpressive jibes at the theatrical world.

Their foolery is suddenly interrupted by Cothurnus, the Masque of Tragedy, who insists on playing his scene. The bored young couple leave, after a bit of futile protest. Cothurnus calls out two simple shepherds, Thyrsis and Corydon, and holds the prompt-book for them. They had not expected to play their scene so soon and believe it inappropriate to do so in a farce-setting: "Our scene requires a wall; we cannot build / A wall of tissue-paper!" Cothurnus, with stern dignity but "quite without feeling, as if he had said the same words many times before,"[6] says, "One wall is like another. . . . Play the play!" (25–26).

The shepherds indulge in pleasant pastoral comment about their sheep, and Corydon suggests that they make a song. Thyrsis wishes to agree but is prompted by Cothurnus to deliver the lines in Cothurnus's book: "I know a game worth two of that! / Let's gather rocks, and build a wall between us; / And say that over there belongs to me, / And over here to you!" (27). They weave their wall with colored crepe paper ribbons. Thyrsis soon thinks it "a silly game" and prefers to make the song Corydon had suggested. Corydon has to be prompted to declare: "How do I know this isn't a trick / To get upon my land?" (28); but, since he insists upon viewing Thyrsis's idea with suspicion, their separation continues. Then Corydon notices that ". . . all the water / Is on your side of the wall, and the sheep are thirsty. / I hadn't thought of that" (29). Thyrsis retaliates by being stubborn and selfish. Anger and suspicion increase. Yet for the time—since, as Corydon says,

>   it's only
> A game, you know . . .
>   . . . a pretty serious game
> It's getting to be, when one of us is willing
> To let the sheep go thirsty for the sake of it— (30)

they are able to keep their heads and proceed to "reach out their arms to each other across the wall," until Cothurnus forces Thyrsis to express suspicion again. Now Corydon feels that the wall between them has turned his comrade into a stranger, and Thyrsis's invitation to bring the sheep over for water makes Corydon suspect his sincerity. Columbine reappears for an instant to get her hat, and her comment—"Really, you know, you two / Are awfully funny!" (32)—has a pathetically ironic, ironically sinister implication.

Presently Corydon discovers jewels on his land and makes Thyrsis envious. Thyrsis fails to find jewels but comes upon the root of a black weed. When Corydon becomes thirsty, they strike a bargain: a bowl of jewels for a bowl of water. Each is greedy and treacherous: Thyrsis has poisoned the water with the black root, and Corydon has "necklaces" ready to strangle Thyrsis so that he can regain his jewels. He threatens Thyrsis: "For every drop you spill I'll have a stone back / Out of this chain" (40). Thyrsis's measured, stony reply is ominous: "I shall not spill a drop." The strangling and the poisoning proceed simultaneously. Thyrsis dies. Corydon, blind and numbed with deadly cold, stumbles and gropes, muttering incoherently, intending to come over the wall—"I want to be near you." Finally he "strides through the frail papers . . . without knowing it" (41). Begging for a bit of his fellow's cloak, he falls upon Thyrsis's body and dies as he draws a corner of the cloak over his shoulders.

After a pause just long enough for mingled pity and indignation to take effect on the audience, Cothurnus "closes the prompt-book with a bang." He leaves, after shoving the table over the bodies, callously "pushing in their feet and hands with his boot" (42), and pulling the cloth so that the bodies can be seen by the audience but not by people on the stage. When Pierrot and Columbine then return, she complains that the set has been disarranged; but Pierrot thinks "it rather diverting / The way it is." She catches sight of the dead bodies and screams. As they examine the corpses, she says, "How curious to strangle him like that, / With colored paper ribbons." Pierrot replies, "Yes, and yet / I dare say he is just as dead." He wants Cothurnus to drag the bodies out; the audience "wouldn't stand for" their eating with the corpses under the table. Off stage Cothurnus advises him to pull the tablecloth down and hide the bodies—"The audience will forget" (43). So the Harlequin characters hide the bodies from the spectators, "then merrily set their bowls back on the table, . . . and begin the play exactly as before. . . . 'Pierrot, a macaroon,—I cannot *live* without a macaroon!'"

Part of the effect of *Aria da Capo* arises from the contrast of the harlequinade and the pastoral—of the frivolous and the serious— neither one close to the "realism" of modern daily life but following ancient dramatic modes. Bored, flighty Pierrot and silly Columbine are set against the shepherds in the abstract dramatic scheme. Each pair, in its own way, represents Mankind—that is, different aspects of the human character. The mad moderns are an updated version of New-Gyse and Now-A-Days in the old morality. Man's workaday character in the world of labor and livelihood is represented by Corydon and Thyrsis—who ought by pastoral tradition to be leading Arcadian lives, but who are, though reluctantly, developing instead separatism, private property, suspicion, selfishness, hatred, cunning, and a will to murder. The pathos is increased by the fact that they are naturally sweet and good; it is not easy for them to learn the "parts" they must "play." Although the death-scene will be played again and again, the young clowns will continue, after only a pause, their blasé love-banter.

Millay's technique allows the juxtaposition of the two differing scenes. It is an expressionistic technique, which, to project the dramatic theme, uses a symbolic playhouse where, fantastically, grotesquely, and allegorically, play is transformed to reality; and those who were "acting" find themselves murdered. The mingling of "illusion" and "reality" accounts for the peculiar impact of the play. One must see things in terms of a circle: an audience of real people in a theater are viewing a play representing a theater where scenes are portrayed by actors who reluctantly take unwelcome "parts" which they find to be "real."

Millay told Grace King that she had conceived the idea of *Aria da Capo* as early as 1916. She had explained the idea to John Reed before he had left for Russia in 1918,[7] and in 1918 Floyd Dell knew she was working on the play.[8] *Aria da Capo* is one of many modern plays in the harlequinade tradition. Patton has identified several with some similarity to Millay's work. Probably the most significant is Robert Emmons Rogers's *Behind a Watteau Picture,* produced at the Greenwich Village Theatre in November 1917, which combines "real" people with harlequinade characters. After the Poet and the Marquis have killed each other, their bodies are treated roughly: "The Negroes drag the bodies roughly across the grass and dump them into the open grave."[9]

Patton also places *Aria da Capo* in relation to other symbolic, antirealistic plays of the art theater of the time. Rostand had taken steps in the anti-realistic direction with *Les Romanesques,* in which Millay had played at Vassar. *The Yellow Jacket,* an imitation of Chinese drama by Hazelton and Benrimo, which Millay had thought "altogether ravishing" in 1917, has a "chorus" or "prompter" on the stage during the action, lets the audience see the changing of settings, and uses make-believe stage properties. Cloyd Head's completely stylized *Grotesques,* a verse play of 1915, also had a commentator; symbolic characters, costumes, and settings; and figures of a marionette quality. Millay was familiar with Kreymborg's *Plays for Poet-Mimes,* free-verse plays with stylized setting, characterization, and action.[10] To these one might add Benavente's *Bonds of Interest,* in which the characters are puppets. Millay had played Benavente's Columbine. Finally, Wallace Stevens had used verse in an effective dramatic way in his symbolic one-act play *Three Travelers Watch a Sunrise,* published in *Poetry* in 1916. It is reasonable to think, therefore, that being in the world of the art theater helped Millay to perceive the means by which her concept of the play could be translated into effective dramatic action.

For *Aria da Capo* she used blank verse with only occasional variations. The movement is less formal and regular when Pierrot and Columbine are talking than in the shepherds' dialogue. The inconsequential effect of the harlequinade dialogue is reinforced by the large number of very short grammatical units, the small number of run-on lines, and the colloquial vocabulary (although at times there is just a touch of the archaic-poetic). The speeches of Pierrot when Cothurnus appears are very colloquial and contrast with the dignified tone of Cothurnus. The shepherds have a larger percentage of longer sentences to speak than have the other characters, and more than 40 percent of their lines are run-on, a proportion twice as great as that in the harlequinade. The beginning of their dialogue about the sheep is serious, dignified, rather lyrical; but during their "game" they speak excitedly, almost like boys. Then when indignation overcomes them, their insinuations of double-dealing are expressed in colloquial language: "I'll say you had an eye out / For lots of little things, my innocent friend, / When I said, 'Let us make a song,' and you said, / 'I know a game worth two of that!' " (30). The longer sentences and the run-on lines chiefly set off the shepherds' speeches from the triviality of the harlequinade. As the double killing draws near, the regularity of the iambic meter increases. In sum, Millay varies her verse with appropriate skill in the several parts of the play. Furthermore, whatever suggestions she may have picked up from the example of other dramatists, *Aria da Capo* is a highly original play.

Alexander Woollcott reviewed it soon after it opened. Although he spoke of it as a "fairly enigmatic piece," he advised his readers to see it, for he considered it, aside from limitations of production and performance, "the most beautiful and most interesting play in the English language now to be seen in New York."[11] He regarded it as an antiwar play, and so did most other critics.[12] But "antiwar play" is an inadequate description; Cook came nearer the mark in calling it "a devastating indictment of man's folly, his greed, his quarrels, his war-like games." This broader interpretation is favored also by Patton, who treats the drama as a "telling comment on human treachery and self-betrayal, which often nurture war because they ignore human need and human love."[13] *Aria da Capo* reads a deeper lesson than an antiwar play, for Millay chose to express what is representative and everlasting; the play has more in common with the tales of Cain and Abel and of Everyman than with most twentieth-century antiwar literature.

Aria da Capo is an example of symbolic and expressionistic drama, occupying a position somewhere between the work of Maeterlinck and Wilder. Frank Shay said in 1922 that *Aria* and O'Neill's *Emperor Jones* represented "the high accomplishments of the art theatre in America,"[14] and Millay herself was proud of her play. She wrote in a letter in 1947 that, though it had imperfections (perhaps the commonplace satire on the arts in the first five pages), "it was written for the theatre" and "to see it well played is an unforgettable experience." It has retained unusual popularity for more than sixty years: it has often been reprinted, has had many productions, and is still being produced regularly. The high place of *Aria da Capo* in American poetic drama illustrates very well how certain plays "by the use of symbols escape over the boundaries of realism into the evergreen and limitless fields of poetic truth."[15]

The Lamp and the Bell

The Vassar College Alumnae Association commissioned Millay to write a play for its fiftieth anniversary celebration on 18 June 1921. With her sister Kathleen, she "worked out the idea" of using the fairy tale "Rose White and Rose Red" as the basis of her play; and she finished the play, *The Lamp and the Bell*, by 18 March 1921.

The play is a shrewd practical application of materials to meet the needs of the occasion. Millay had very clear ideas of these needs: "It's written in the first place for Vassar College, in the second place it's written to be played out of doors, as spectacularly as possible, & in a foreign country & medieval times because in that way you can use more brilliant costumes. . . ." She saw very clearly, too, shortcomings of her work, which she perhaps exaggerated:

. . . in the third place I haven't had time to work it over at all, in the fourth place it's full of anachronisms which I haven't had time to look up & put right, & in the fifth place it's a frank shameless imitation of the Elizabethan dramas, in style, conversation & everything . . .

Millay was acutely aware of the difference between such an imitative costume drama as this one and experimental works like *Aria da Capo* and others favored by the Provincetown. She cautioned Norma not to let any Provincetown Players read it: "they would hate it, & make fun of it, & old Djuna Barnes would rag you about it, hoping it would get to me."

The play opens in a workmanlike way. A brief conversational prologue makes the reader aware of the situation: a widower king with a young daughter is marrying a woman with a daughter; the two girls are to grow up as playmates and friends. The systematic exposition of Act I introduces the characters and the situation at the court of Fiori four years after the king's remarriage. The characters are Fidelio the Jester, a melancholy wit and lutanist; Bianca, the Queen's sweet daughter; Beatrice, "Rose Red," the bolder, more independent daughter of the King; Francesca, a girl in love with Guido, illegitimate nephew to the King. Guido argues with Fidelio, has no ear for music, and seems heavy and ill-tempered.

The two girls have developed a passionate devotion for each other. It is Bianca who raises the crucial question of who will marry first and whether they will always remain friends. Beatrice's superior strength is shown; she is tender and protective toward Bianca. The nature of the Queen and the King remains to be revealed. Queen Octavia, like the traditional stepmother, is sharp-natured while the King is rational and tolerant. She thinks it not good for two girls to be so much together; the King considers it natural. Yet he allows her to send Bianca away.

Four months later Beatrice and visiting King Mario are falling in love with each other—while Guido bitterly watches them, her hatred of him drawing him to her. Francesca still loves Guido but he no longer cares for her. Vigorous Beatrice, rather a tomboy, resembles Rosalind of *As You Like It.* Guido tells the Queen that she had better get her daughter home so that Bianca, with her attractive weakness, may marry a king. He, of course, desires to prevent Beatrice's marriage, and he has judged Octavia's ambition well, for she has already summoned Bianca.

Act III opens in the following summer. A bridal song is being sung; the courtiers and ladies, grumbling and joking, bring flowers. The first scene is mainly spectacle and song. Bianca, the bride-to-be, asks Beatrice her opinion of Mario. There is sharp irony here, for in reply to Bianca's comment—"I could not bear / To wed a man that was displeasing to you"—Beatrice assures her: "You could not find / In Christendom a man would please me more" (*Three Plays*, 93). They are still devoted friends, and Bianca vows never to forget Beatrice: "You are a burning lamp to me, a flame / The wind cannot blow out, and I shall hold you / High in my hand against whatever darkness." Beatrice replies: "You are to me a silver bell in a tower, / And when it rings I know I am near home" (95).

Beatrice, a generous and understanding young woman, does not blame Mario for having given his love to Bianca—"Because you loved me once a little and now / Love somebody else much more. The going of love / Is no less honest than the coming of it. / It is a human thing" (96). One now finds out that, ironically, before Beatrice could tell Bianca of her romance with Mario, Bianca by her first words on her return showed that she loved him; she had already seen him. Beatrice gave up her own hopes, but could be happy in the love of her friend. Mario honors her for courage and nobility, but he loves Bianca for her gentleness. He wishes to shelter her, but Beatrice needs no shelter.

Another great spectacle follows—a wedding dance, during which the King dies. When the court discover his death, the people are confused. (The dramaturgy is rather crude and hurried here.) Bianca can also be noble; on her wedding night she sends Mario away so that she may be with her friend in her sorrow—a situation reminiscent of Portia on her bridal day.

Five years elapse between Acts III and IV. In a market scene, one learns that Queen Beatrice has been injured while hunting—and that King Mario is dead. Later the widowed Bianca is taunted by her mother; why has Beatrice not come to her? Bianca is sure there must be a good reason, but her mother insists that Beatrice had loved Mario. Bianca will not believe it. She goes to visit Beatrice—to "let her lay her quiet on my heart" (123).

When Bianca arrives, Beatrice explains that she has been ill, but asks her to leave; though she still loves her, she has wronged her. Thinking of what her mother said, Bianca asks, "Then is it true?" With relief, Beatrice says, "Yes"; then, mistaking the point of their talk, she tells how, after being wounded by brigands, she thrust at a rider—and killed Mario! Bianca rushes off, and Beatrice "falls unconscious to the floor" (128).

The final test of friendship comes two years later, with Act V, which opens with forebodings. Guido is plotting to take the throne. He still desires Beatrice, and Francesca loves him still. Upon hearing that Bianca is dying, Beatrice starts away but is seized by soldiers. Guido will let her go to Bianca only on condition that she give herself to him upon returning. She finally agrees:

> This foolish body,
> This body is not I! There is no I,
> Saving the need I have to go to her! (141)

Bianca, fearing she may die before her friend comes, leaves a message: her two children are Beatrice's—and "all's well 'twixt her and me" (142). Soon Beatrice enters—and Bianca, throwing her arms about her neck, dies.

Integrity has been saved and friendship vindicated; and the good queen receives further recompense. Fidelio announces that Guido is dead, stabbed in the back, and Francesca drowned, "Who last was seen a-listening like a ghost / At the door of the dungeon" (145). Also, the people of Fiori rose up and swept away Guido's men. A further hopeful note is heard. After receiving Bianca's message, Beatrice says "slowly and with great content":

> She is returned
> From her long silence, and rings out above me
> Like a silver bell!—Let us go back, Fidelio,
> And gather up the fallen stones, and build us
> Another tower. (147)

The Lamp and the Bell, with its five acts, was Millay's most ambitious early dramatic undertaking; her prior plays had only one act. It was skillfully contrived for the occasion. The cast was made large by creating, besides the members of the Court, the strolling players of the pantomime and the villagers of Fiori. Spectacle and music are prominent, especially in II.ii, the pantomime scene; III.i, the flower-gathering scene; III.iv, the wedding dance; and IV.i, the Fiori market scene.

Millay thought the play well constructed. Patton points out that the construction involves two triangles, each with two women and a man: (1) Francesca-Guido-Beatrice and (2) Beatrice-Mario-Bianca. In both triangles the rejected woman kills the man, but one killing occurs by accident, the other for revenge. Suspense is well achieved regarding two important questions: Whose wedding is being prepared for? Who killed Mario? As Millay indicated, many elements of the play come from the Elizabethan drama.[16]

The dialogue has a certain amount of wit; the diction is pleasantly simple and natural; the verse is well managed and more homogeneous and more original than that of *The Princess Marries the Page.* But, as Millay wrote in 1947, it "seldom rises above the merely competent." The play has elements of pathos and irony, yet the tragic effect is weakened by the pageantlike succession of scenes spread out over an action covering more than a dozen years and by some dependence on the spectacular and melodramatic. Guido seems a pasteboard villain, and the end is too patly contrived.[17] Nevertheless, ideals of unselfish love and friendship are warmly but unsentimentally revealed at the core of the play.

The King's Henchman

The King's Henchman, Millay's opera libretto, is a story of divided loyalties, of love versus honor. King Eadgar of the West Saxons sends

his foster-brother Aethelwold to Devon to assess the suitability of
Aelfrida, daughter of the Thane of Devon, for the queenship. If she is
suitable, he is to woo and win her for the King. A doughty young
warrior, Aethelwold is completely devoted to Eadgar, has saved his life
from a wild boar, is praised for his loyalty, and is not interested in
women. People say he will bring the King's "shilling," his betrothed,
safely back. Aethelwold is loath to go on the King's errand, for "So
many dry leaves in a ditch they are to me, / The whispering girls . . ."
(26). But the King, a widower, wishes to marry again and prefers to
send a trusty man who is not easily impressed.

This material, the exposition of the play, is brought out in the
closing hours of a banquet for which Millay created an excellently
jocular and convivial atmosphere. Especially effective are the account of
the brothers and the boar, and the vigorous chorus "Oh, Caesar, great
wert thou!"

Act II takes place on All Hallow's Eve in a misty forest of Devonshire
where Aethelwold and Maccus, warrior-servant and harper, have lost
their way. While Maccus searches for their men, Aethelwold sleeps.
There beautiful Aelfrida comes to "seek in spell and rune . . . / Her
lover that is to be" (49). Seeing Aethelwold asleep, she loses her heart to
him; and, as soon as he wakes and sees her, he is smitten. Aethelwold
betrays his brother, sending Maccus back to report that the daughter of
the Thane of Devon is "nothing fair," unfit for the King—but that he
himself will remain and marry her because her father is rich.

Act III reveals the married couple the following spring. Aethelwold
is unhappy because of his guilt and his separation from warrior's work,
yet still "love's churl" (85); Aelfrida is testily preoccupied with her
father's household, sick of living at home with a mind "full of thimbles
and churns" (86). She is impatient for her husband to take her to
the Court at Winchester where she would enjoy prestige and a fine
house. He, of course, cannot take her there. When he tempts her to go
to Ghent in Flanders to buy new clothes, she is enthusiastic. He, too, is
eager to leave England, though regretful when he thinks of bidding
farewell to its heaths and downs. Hope of happier times and places
excites them as they sing: "Oh, let us wander far! Oh, let us live
forever! / The world is wide, and we are hale, and we are young!" (98).

At this moment, Maccus arrives to announce that the King is approaching—simply to pay his brother a visit. Aethelwold sees three riders coming: the King, and Shame, and Doom. Trying to make Aelfrida understand his danger, he—imprudently—tells her how he came as the King's henchman to woo her for the King and how he lied and betrayed his brother. She is tempted by the thought of the lost queenship, but she agrees to remain in her bower disguised as an ugly woman—then is persuaded by her servant Ase not to, in order to "drop thy silver shell, to pick up the gold one" (111).

The king is cordial to Aethelwold, sympathetic for his having wed "a maid no other man would have . . ." (118). Aethelwold suffers, for his sin and for thinking of riding with Eadgar into Wales to fight again; and Eadgar sees that all is not well with him. When the King goes to visit his brother's wife, who he is told is ailing in her bower, Aelfrida steps out, richly dressed and "amazingly beautiful" (123). Eadgar realizes the truth—is bewildered, saddened. . . . Whom, in his whole kingdom, can he trust, if Aethelwold is false? In bitterness, shame, despair, Aethelwold slays himself. All scorn Aelfrida. They sing the Lament for the Untimely Dead: Life goes on, men's many activities, of ax and boat and horse—"and thou liest here." The play ends with a Chorus of People:

> Woe—lo—woe!
> Hearest thou the wind in the tree?
> He that spoke but now is no longer in the room.
> Forth-faréd is he.

Both author and composer of the opera were praised because they had made no concession by inserting arias that would attract the public. "It is almost incontestable that the lyric drama of Miss Millay and Mr. Taylor is the greatest American opera so far. . . ."[18] Millay's diction troubled some critics, however. In the interest of authenticity she had used a strongly Saxon vocabulary, limiting herself to words some form of which was in use before the Norman Conquest. To do this seemed to some no more than a stunt in archaism or, as Lee Simonson wrote, "the verbal masquerade of a poetess in a farthingale." He objected to the "vocal brambles" of the text and claimed that the opera proved the inferiority of English to Italian and French for singing.[19] Such objections were authoritatively answered by Edward Johnson, the tenor who sang the part of Aethelwold. He commended its "beautiful English libretto, . . . singable, and soft and welcome to the ear," its lack of triteness and banality, and also its sense of reality and psychological accuracy.[20]

There is much to commend in *The King's Henchman*. The contrasting characters of the brothers and the objectionable quality of Aelfrida are excellently revealed. Skillful dramaturgy created the theatrical entrance of Aelfrida at the door of her bower, the suicide of Aethelwold rather than his death at Eadgar's hands as in the source, and Maccus's fierce bidding of Aelfrida to stand back from Aethelwold's body. The atmosphere of each act is consistently established: the masculinity of Act I, the other-worldly lyricism of Act II, and the mixture of romance and irritable domesticity in Act III. The verse is varied with remarkable skill, from the opening in "Old English" alliterative measures, through the strongly rhythmic choruses, the discursive passages expressing the purposes and moods of the characters, and the love-duet with its fluctuations of line-length and rhyme, to the stark lament at the close. The drama has a directness and simplicity of plot suitable to opera; and the poetry, though naturally not so intense as Millay's lyrics, abounds in imagery. The diction is prevailingly concrete; the style, frequently natural and colloquial.[21]

Although Millay gave the enchanting power of love its full due, the main focus of the play, as Patton emphasizes (169–71), is upon the integrity of the self. When Aethelwold violates his code of honor, betraying himself as well as his brother, his act leads to further betrayal: his deception opens the way for the selfish greed of Aelfrida. In his anguished crisis of realization, his only means of redemption is to drive his sword through his own heart.

Chapter Five

"The Rich and Varied Voices"

The Buck in the Snow

With *The Buck in the Snow* Millay demonstrated further poetic experimentation. Untermeyer praised her "interesting experiments": "the lengthening and increased flexibility of her line"; the creating of "an unusual set of suspensions and cadences by combining free verse and, occasionally, prose rhythms with balanced measures."[1] Minot (155) points to Millay's development of a new "speaking voice" expressed "in longer, freer, more irregular lines both in meter and in free verse." Nearly half of the shorter lyrics in the volume have an irregular verse movement that, at first glance, looks like free verse; but the reader soon discovers blossoms of rhyme starring the lines that the poet, with instinctive sureness, has varied in length. The variety of rhythms is notable: dactylic-anapestic feet are numerous though they do not outnumber the iambic-trochaic. In these works—such as "Mist in the Valley," "The Pigeons," "The Buck in the Snow," and "On First Having Heard the Skylark"—the assured, experienced poet is at the peak of her art.

Representative of her times, Millay embraced the idea of an indifferent universe. In "To the Wife of a Sick Friend," a tribute to Arthur Ficke,[2] she speaks of "the cave wherein we wander lost" (*CP,* 209), illuminated by the man-candle which must be sheltered from the wind of death; if it is extinguished, the poet and Mrs. Ficke will be left in "unmitigated dark." In "Dirge without Music" all fine persons must go "into the darkness." Without Christian hope of immortality, "I am not resigned" (*CP,* 240), she writes. "Moriturus" (*CP,* 199–207) explains the terms on which she might "dicker with dying": she would like the peace of death without the pains of the body, yet still without giving up consciousness and sensation. With a rush of images she makes the concept of death seem insignificant and, blending "the lightly comic and the serious," ends by giving death a witty dismissal.[3] But death is scarcely an insignificant "nothing"; it is utter negation of all that Millay values. Optimistic ideas of any sort of immortality she brushes aside as visions—"the grave's derisions"—and she insists that life at its worst is worth contention. In the last ten stanzas she creates a vividly ugly picture of helpless old age but declares that such a life with all its indignities is preferable to death's "nothing good." The sonnet "Not that it matters" (CP, 625) also assumes an indifferent universe: only love, like a jewel scratched from a tomb, can stand out—temporarily—against death.

The volume contains a group of five poems on the theme of injustice. Although in "Renascence" she had felt all sin and pain, the Sacco-Vanzetti experience brought directly home to her the bitterness of injustice, the realities of harshness, prejudice, and suffering therefrom—so that she wrote in "The Anguish": "The anguish of the world is on my tongue. / My bowl is filled to the brim with it; there is more than I can eat" (CP, 229). Even before the execution she wrote "Justice Denied in Massachusetts," a farmer's poem, thoroughly agricultural, by one who knows that quack grass flourishes in rainy weather. It is based on the metaphor Justice is Light; so she laments the blighted crops—the ruined traditions of justice and free speech—under the cloud of injustice. To her it seemed a permanent darkening of America. "Hangman's Oak" is a balladlike poem with much variation of meter and line length; here the Sacco-Vanzetti affair is transposed into a real lynching. Based on the metaphor of an indelible stain: "Stained with these grapes I shall lie down to die" (CP, 234), "Wine from These Grapes" depends in part for its effect upon the reader's recollection of "trampling out the vintage where the grapes of wrath are stored." Evidently the Sacco-Vanzetti affair gave Millay a permanent conviction that the times were out of joint—a feeling of bitter disillusionment, distrust, and alienation.

Yet other poems strongly assert her admiration of daring and hardihood, her feeling that intangibles like love, beauty, magnanimity, and courage have value, and her conviction that the life-experience is essentially good. The sonnet "Life, were thy pains as are the pains of hell" (CP, 623) upholds the value of living, no matter how much suffering is entailed, and seems to be the utterance of an enraptured vitalist to whom earthly joys are heavenly. In "The Bobolink" Millay admires the bird as an epitome of daring and gallantry, ignoring the precariousness of life; and in "The Hawkweed" she favors the resistance of the beautiful weed to agricultural improvement.

The great pictorial qualities of her poetry appear frequently in *The Buck in the Snow*. The title poem reminded Cook of "the soft, the subdued, but fluid movement of a Japanese print. . . ."[4] One who knows northern winters feels at once that all the details of the picture are exactly right. Millay used her skill to slow up the *l*-crammed line showing the deer leaving the orchard—"Tails up, with long leaps lovely and slow" (*CP*, 228)—to point, by inversion, with deliberate finality at the dying buck, all his intense vitality concentrated in *wild* and *scalding*: "Now lies he here, his wild blood scalding the snow"—and to picture the doe hiding "under the heavy hemlocks," an incarnation of puzzled, precarious life—"Life, looking out attentive from the eyes of the doe."[5] Both verse movement and alliteration are beautifully controlled. The connotative value of "feather of snow" can scarcely be calculated, but the sense of the chill muffling whiteness is emphasized by ending five of the twelve lines with *snow*.

Another striking pictorial poem is the imagistic "Pueblo Pot," which presents red-shafted flickers "Wrenching the indigo berry from the shedding woodbine with strong ebony beak" (*CP*, 250). (The musical line is made emphatic by the vigorous alliteration.) The birds cannot restore the beauty of the Indian pot lying in shards; but they substitute for it another perfect beauty.

The Buck in the Snow deals as much with the past remembered as with the dramatic present. Several poems seem to have European settings. The remarkable "Cameo" represents a memory of lovers on a beach— perhaps Millay and her French lover. "O troubled forms, O early love unfortunate and hard, / Time has estranged you into a jewel cold and pure . . ." (*CP*, 246). Though the exact words and the pain of the lovers are lost, the incident persists in memory "like a scene cut in cameo." "To a Musician" and "The Pigeons" also concern the past, but in them the estrangement of time has not been completed—a situation "now" and "today" is also touched on. The pigeons symbolizing the past are presented onomatopoetically: "How they conversed throughout the afternoon in their monotonous voices never for a moment still"—but the painter drove them away. The poet visualizes him continuing to paint "in a quiet room, empty of the past, . . . thinking of me no more"; but she, not empty of the past but regretful for having left him, must "Walk in a noise of yesterday and of the days before, / Walk in a cloud of wings intolerable . . ." (CP, 226–27). "Portrait," which is about Edmund Wilson reading to her in the Village days,[6] is partly based on memories but also touches an immediate present.

Other poems concerning the past are "Memory of Cassis," "The Road to Avrillé," and "Song," which states that summer "is gone again like a jeweled fish from the hand" (CP, 208). This muted lyric with a fine pattern of alliteration is one of her most accomplished creations. As Millay reached her middle thirties, she became more involved with her past, with experiences irrevocably gone—save in the memory. The transcience of things assailed by devouring time makes the memories more significant.

The old intensity of her response to life is projected into her remembrance of "On First Having Heard the Skylark," when she was overwhelmed by "his sweet crying like a crystal dart." Then she saw the bird, "A dark articulate atom in the mute enormous blue . . ." (CP, 256); and calling him "Blithe Spirit!" she fell and ". . . lay among the foreign daisies pink and small. . . ." She wept because, joined with her rapture in the notes, there rushed upon her all her memories of the skylark as the subject of immortal poems. But the implication of the first lines of the poem is that she would not have responded so if she had known then that the lark had "A wing of earth, with the warm loam / Closely acquainted. . . ." The poet's need to keep in touch with earth is expressed in the sonnet "Grow not too high" (CP, 624). Earth must furnish the sustenance of the tree of poetry: "Earth's fiery core alone can feed the bough / That blooms between Orion and the Plough." Presumably that starry bough of poetry must be connected with struggling and suffering earth. But earth brings to sensitive spirits the spring-raptures of "Northern April" (CP, 219), which might be called a "God's World" of a dozen years after. A poem with an original verse-pattern, it suggests the almost unbearable thrill of renewed activity after winter, its repetitions conveying the nigh-frantic feeling of the winter-paled who "emerge like yellow grass."

The volume closes with the Shakespearean sonnet "On Hearing a Symphony of Beethoven," a tribute to the power of great music to create an enchanted and perfect world in which the enraptured listener would wish to remain forever. From line 5 on, Millay has in mind the story of the Sleeping Beauty. In the sestet the poet herself becomes metaphorically the city "spell-bound under the aging sun, / Music my rampart, and my only one" (*CP,* 629).[7] So music—could the wish be granted—would replace the traditional thorn hedge as a defense against an intrusive world of change, uncertainty, and evil.

The Buck in the Snow does not contain novelties of the author's thought or personality, but it is more mature, less clever, and more thoughtful, than her earlier collections; and it has much that in technical respects is fresh and interesting.

Fatal Interview

The sequence of fifty-two Shakespearean sonnets published in April 1931 as *Fatal Interview* Millay originally intended to issue under the title *Twice Required,* a phrase from Sonnet 14: "Since of no creature living the last breath / Is twice required. . . ." In fact, a publisher's dummy containing three sonnets was printed with that title. But 1931 was Donne's tercentenary year, and it was decided, according to Norma Millay, to change the title, the epigraph of the volume being taken from Donne's "Elegy 16": "By our first strange and fatall interview, / By all desires which thereof did ensue." The new title was a better one; but it implies no connection between Donne's work and Millay's sonnets.

Fatal Interview presents a woman's responses to a passionate love affair from first attraction through the ecstasies of consummation to the sorrows of breaking up (because the lover grows cold) and eventually to resignation. Sonnets 1 and 52 deal with the legend of Selene and Endymion, the moon-goddess and the handsome mortal with whom she fell in love. Between these sonnets are fifty others which imply a story and express a woman's feelings as she passes through a love affair that probably has considerable correspondence to that of Millay and Dillon. When more information becomes available, the degree of correspondence may be determined. But it seems likely, since their affair continued after the fall of 1930, that *Fatal Interview* is not an exact autobiographical record but that the poet made alterations to construct a work more in accord with her literary purposes, her pattern having been laid down by the myth of Selene and Endymion.

The speaker in Sonnet 1 is a goddess, a being immune from the doom of mankind (and identified in Sonnet 52 as Selene). In Sonnet 2, however, it is no goddess but an American woman who says: "I shall forget before the flickers mate / Your look that is today my east and west." The eyes of the man, especially distinctive and irresistible, are mentioned not only in Sonnets 1 and 2 but also in 4 ("eyed with stars") and 9 ("disturbing eyes. . . . remembered morning stars"). In Sonnets 2, 4, and 5 love is represented as a disease ("the sick disorder in my flesh"—Sonnet 4) which she cannot conceal.

With Sonnet 6 there is a sudden shift, and she blames the man for ignoring her on account of his "pale preoccupation with the dead" heroines of old love stories. It is hard to tell whether this sonnet is a dramatic monologue or a soliloquy, but in any case it expresses her impatience with the oblivious, unresponsive man. He alone could save her from being drowned in love (Sonnet 7), but she does not expect him to. Her mood shifts then from self-pity to scornful accusation as she warns him how short life is. But she cannot free herself from loving and, against her own philosophy of freedom, is driven to possessiveness. The reader is to suppose that her sweet and guileless offer of "love in the open hand" (Sonnet 11) wins him at last, for Sonnet 12 expresses the raptures of consummation. She is a mortal woman whose bed Zeus himself has honored ("Enraptured in his great embrace I lie"), and she foresees having a demigod for a son.

The next eight sonnets present her shifting moods: hatred of separation, insatiable desire, foreboding that love will betray her, praise of the lover, first regrets, the repulsion-fascination of being love's helpless prisoner and finally, in Sonnet 20, a warning to herself that continuance of the beautiful experience cannot be assured. Beauty is not to be bought: "Beauty beyond all feathers that have flown / Is free; you shall not hood her to your wrist. . . ."

The next sonnet indicates a separation of the lovers—which proves unendurable to her. The affair is renewed with Sonnet 25. She is willing to disregard "wrath and scorn" as long as the experience is beautiful;

and she is proud to be "heedless and wilful," like the "treacherous queens" of old who bore "Love like a burning city in the breast" (Sonnet 26). Sonnets 27 to and including 30 dwell on the raptures of love, too soon ended by dawn; the *carpe diem* theme appears in 28 and 29. Sonnets 29 to 32 assert more idealistically the lasting excellence of love in the face of destroying time. Sonnet 33 is premonitory of grief and loss: "Desolate dreams pursue me out of sleep; / Weeping I wake; waking, I weep, I weep." Then in Sonnet 34 the lover is chidden for voicing doubts which are likely to cause the death of their love; very fervently she begs, "Believe that I shall love you till I die; / Believe. . . ." This reaction is the beginning of the end, for she too has doubts of his constancy (Sonnet 35); she finds him wavering (Sonnet 36), envisions their love-city destroyed (Sonnet 37), and quotes his excuses for ending their love (Sonnet 38), to which she replies: "Oh, tortured voice, be still! / Spare me your premise: leave me when you will." The decisive break comes in Sonnet 39, where her pride and bitterness flash out: "Love me no more, now let the god depart, / If love be grown so bitter to your tongue!"

Yet she still has a generous spirit, and although in the remaining sonnets she has ups and downs of feeling—for the pangs of readjustment are severe before she achieves resignation—she refuses to disparage him; whatever pain she suffers now, she has had an exalting experience (Sonnet 45). And she insists on sincerity, for she is too idealistic to compromise or temporize. Sonnet 52 implies a parallel between this devastating love affair and that of Selene and Endymion. Millay's sympathy goes out to Selene suffering endless pain. The mortal lover remains oblivious, sleeping: no man, however magnificent he may be, can understand a woman's anguish and "altered state" that come of such an affair.[8]

Millay achieved universality in this sonnet sequence, as Patricia Klemans indicates, "by interweaving the woman's experience with classical myth, traditional love literature, and nature."[9] The first two of these elements appear not only in Sonnets 1 and 52 but also in 6, 12, 15, 16, and 26. Nature, with its predictable constancy and its unpredictable vicissitudes, offers object lessons throughout. Awareness of the passing seasons and of what they will do to alter love is brought out in Sonnet 2. When the affair does begin to wane, her memory of her

frost-ruined garden—"Though summer's rife and the warm rose in
season" (Sonnet 35)—suggests the coming winter of love. Similarly the
autumnal imagery of Sonnet 36, where "the island women stand / In
gardens stripped and scattered, peering north, / With dahlia tubers
dripping from the hand," heightens the expectation of stormy times
ahead. After the break-up has occurred, she wishes in Sonnet 43 for no
season to exist except "surly Winter," even though it is still summer, so
wintry is her heart. And in Sonnet 46, looking back (as it were, to
Sonnet 2), with imagery of bud, flower, and seed, and then with
seasonal imagery, again of autumnal frost, she regretfully accepts the
harsh season which has made "the blackened vine" that will produce no
"sunny clusters." Thus love is made to seem susceptible to destruction
like anything else produced by nature, however cherished it may be by
human beings. Nature imagery also appears frequently elsewhere, as in
Sonnets 10, 12, 13, 17, 20, 25, 38, 42, 48, and 49.

To such universalizing elements may be added Millay's use of the
carpe diem theme, with its long literary heritage, in Sonnets 8, 28, 29,[10]
and 31.

On the other hand, many readers felt that in *Fatal Interview,* as in
earlier work, Millay was striking a distinctly modern note.[11] She
stresses the mortality of the lover by representing him as an aggregation
of chemicals (Sonnet 1). The woman of the sonnets is married, it seems,
although she mentions her husband only in Sonnet 2:

> Unscathed, however, from a claw so deep
> Though I should love again I shall not go;
> Along my body, waking while I sleep,
> Sharp to the kiss, cold to the hand as snow,
> The scar of this encounter like a sword
> Will lie between me and my troubled lord.

Sophisticated enough to anticipate an end to her love-sickness, she is
also a modern love-partner in her scorn of conventional coquetry and
calculated "love-tactics"; her feelings are simple, direct, unconcealed:
". . . being like my mother the brown earth, / Fervent and full of gifts
and free from guile" (Sonnet 3). Being anguished, passionate, and
impetuous, she respects "no moral concept" and cares nothing for
"what the tongues / Of tedious men will say, or what the law" (Sonnet
22). She is an utter nonconformist determined to pluck the flower of the
moment.

Although she disapproves of possessiveness between equals in love, she is driven by the old need to possess; instinct conflicts with her sense of honor. Independent and proudly high-minded, this woman exposes herself inevitably, it would seem, to injury and disappointment. Yet even after the bitter opening of Sonnet 39 she can say, "Here is my hand; I bid you from my heart / Fare well, fare very well, be always young." In terms of biography this is a magnanimous statement by a woman of thirty-seven to a man fourteen years younger. It also fits in with the underlying myth, for it represents the desire of the goddess Selene to maintain her lover's beauty forever.

Among the sonnets of *Fatal Interview* there is some inconsistency of style. Minot states that in them Millay uses a "distinctly 'literary' style" and "relies very heavily on images taken from the traditional conventions of the Renaissance love sonnets. . . . The diction is often archaic and usually formal."[12] This is true, but the medieval setting of some sonnets seems to have a bearing on the matter, too. In Sonnet 2 she speaks of "my troubled lord," which may have suggested such a setting, courtly love, and archaic language. Sonnets 3–6 all have medieval material. But in Sonnet 7 there is no indication of period, and in others, such as 10 and 11, the speaker seems to be a modern woman like Millay. Medieval references also appear in Sonnets 18, 19, 24, and 34; but most of the sonnets give no hint of period or are modern in imagery and language. The bulk of the medievalism is in the first half of the sequence. Probably as the poet's excited imagination warmed to the completion of the sequence, she drifted away from the medieval, her mind more attuned to contemporary realism.

In various sonnets exact observation and realistic details become impressive through a triumph of meticulous diction—for example, Sonnets 35, 36, 42, 43, and 46. Reviewers who could not commend the whole sequence found Sonnet 36 the best: here was material unmistakably Millayan and authentic, a remembered scene vividly presented, realistic and completely convincing.

Whatever reservations critics have felt regarding the style, content, or total success of *Fatal Interview,* they have accorded Millay high praise for her exquisite craftsmanship. Reviewers chose most often to quote Sonnet 11—followed by 30, 36, and 52. In my opinion the finest sonnets are 3, 7, 11, 30, 36, and 46. Almost as excellent are 2, 6, 31, 39, 45, and 52. High in technique are 5, 12, 24, and 33. The sonnets are Shakespearean in rhyme scheme, but in about half of them Millay

incorporated the final couplet into a sestet which becomes a firm unit
like the sestet of a Petrarchan sonnet. Notable examples of such sestets
are in sonnets 2 and 3 (already quoted), 5, 11, 39, and 46. The sestets of
2 and 3 are excellent for their rhythm, as are sonnets 6, 11, 39; and 7,
35, and 36 are among those with the unincorporated final couplet.
"The effortless perfection of form, the opulence of language, the felicity
and variety of the music, the poise of the accent, the crescendo and
diminuendo within each sonnet, the unmistakable legato which marks
the control of the great artist—all these are . . . evident. . . ."[13] The
caesura is very successfully managed in the sestet of Sonnet 2 and in
sonnets 7 and 11. Sonnet 11 is a single sentence with its parts most
skillfully disposed, especially in the sestet:

> Love in the open hand, no thing but that,
> Ungemmed, unhidden, wishing not to hurt,
> As one should bring you cowslips in a hat
> Swung from the hand, or apples in her skirt,
> I bring you, calling out as children do:
> "Look what I have!—and these are all for you."

Since *love* is the object of the second *bring,* after the parentheses of lines
9–10 the flow of the verse moves triumphantly to reach a crest with *I
bring you* in line 13, followed by the falling cadence of the rest of the
line, the crescendo of the first two feet of line 14, and then the quiet
close. How effectively the simple country details of the sestet contrast
with the artificiality of the casket, lovers'-knot, and ring of the
octave.[14]

Alliteration and assonance are manificently used in many of the
sonnets, and the couplet of Sonnet 7—"No one but Night, with tears
on her dark face, / Watches beside me in this windy place"—illustrates
her capacity for legato and ritardando. Sonnet 7 contrasts acutely with
Sonnet 6, in which the lines throb with increasingly rapid tempo to
match the impatience of the speaker.

Millay was not exploring any new philosophical territory in this
sequence. The sonnets are those of the feminist, hedonist, and rebel of
earlier volumes—praising beauty, defying Time, glorifying intense
fulfillment while brief life lasts, and also interpreting the emotional
vicissitudes of a woman in love. They do so, however, with greater
poignancy and even more universal appeal than in earlier poems.

Wine from These Grapes

Wine from These Grapes shows Millay's poetry becoming increasingly objective and philosophical. Although the volume contains a few personal, reflective lyrics, it has no personal love poems. The character of the book is determined mainly by the sequence of eighteen sonnets, "Epitaph for the Race of Man"; the relation of mankind to nature, the relation of the individual to society, and the qualities of mankind are the themes not only of the sonnets but also of many of the other lyrics. According to Edmund Wilson, Millay was working in 1920 on a long poem in iambic tetrameter entitled "Epitaph for the Race of Man."[15] In 1928 ten sonnets under that title were published in the *St. Louis Post-Dispatch,* and later Millay added other sonnets to the series. Typescripts in the Ficke Collection at the Yale Library show that she made various alterations and grappled with problems of organization before publishing the sequence in a book.[16]

Sonnets 1–5 constitute a first section, prophesying Man's disappearance and making one see the whole range of earth-history from a far past to a distant future. Sonnets 6–11 show constant activities of Man throughout his history and illustrate his heroic capacities. Sonnets 12–13 are on his alienation from the rest of nature; and the last section, sonnets 14–18, emphasizes his tendencies to self-destruction which will cause the human species to become extinct.

Sonnet 1 is prophetic of a time when the stars will be off their courses and earth will be destroyed by collision with Vega, the great star in the constellation of the Lyre. By that time, however, Man will "be no longer here." Sonnet 2 focuses on the dinosaur, a species which vanished ages ago—"the veined and fertile eggs are long since cold." Sonnet 3 is addressed to the "cretaceous bird," evolutionary successor to dinosaurs at the time when toothed birds died out and both birds and mammals appeared, man among them—man in embryo as early mammal emerging from "the catholic slime . . . and crawling up the shore." According to Sonnet 4, earth simply cannot distinguish Man from other expressions of nature; it has no way to set a special value on Man's unique qualities: laughter, tears, machines, conscience, art, and ability to accumulate knowledge and transmit it. This ability even gave him power, ironically enough, to foresee his own extinction (Sonnet 5). After he is gone, no other tongue in nature will be able to tell of his exploits.

Sonnet 6 is one of the most impressive poems of the sequence. It emphasizes the everlasting stars; "Capella with her golden kids" has not changed since the day of the pyramid-builders, the Egyptian rulers who piously followed their religion because "their will was not to die." The sonnet ends with deft ironical understatement: "And so they had their way; or nearly so." The next four sonnets show Man's courage and endurance portrayed in his struggle at an early stage of civilization in the tropics against other animals for mere survival and in his energy and determination in the face of destruction wrought by earthquake, volcano, and flood. Always he looked to the future:

> . . . I saw him when the sun had set
> In water, leaning on his single oar
> Above his garden faintly glimmering yet . . .
> There bulked the plough, here washed the updrifted weeds . . .
> And scull across his roof and make for shore,
> With twisted face and pocket full of seeds. (Sonnet 10)

In fact, Sonnet 11 suggests that disasters had advantages; they brought out kind feelings, they produced cooperation—"for then it was, his neighbour was his friend."

Sonnet 12 depicts the parallel occupations of farmer and ant—both go out to milk; both must endure the conditions of earth. But they remain separate. Man ignores or perhaps disowns his kinship with other creatures. Nowhere in the rest of creation, according to Sonnet 13 (which seems to parallel Robinson Jeffers's ideas), is there such a disturbing, alien element as Man: although capable of knowledge, as of astronomy, he is narrow and intolerant—". . . flinging a ribald stone / At all endeavor alien to his own."

Sonnet 14, a kind of summary of the previous section, is another tribute to Man's qualities; but it prophesies that fratricidal struggle will cause his extinction. In Sonnet 15, on the same theme, "the questioning mind of Man" explores the universe and fears the eventual annihilation of earth; but Man need not fear this, for he will annihilate himself earlier "in intimate conflict." Man bears a "bad cell," Sonnet 16 conveys, an element of "wild disorder"

> . . . destined to invade
> With angry hordes the true and proper part,
> Till Reason joggles in the headsman's cart,
> And Mania spits from every balustrade.

This figure, although developed as a picture of revolution, is ultimately Platonic: reason, which ought to rule in the harmonious personality, is overthrown by will and appetite. In fact, Greed is Man's betrayer. Sonnet 17 explains Man's self-destruction with an elaborate metaphor: "Only the diamond and the diamond's dust / Can render up the diamond unto man. . . ." And Man, able to survive all outward assaults, similarly destroys himself, "being split along the vein by his own kind." The last sonnet in the series envisages Man "cut down to spring no more, . . . even in his infancy cut down. . . ." And by what power? ". . . Whose the heavy blade? . . . / Strive not to speak, poor scattered mouth; I know."

Millay evidently did not intend the sequence to be regarded as a gloomy, dispiriting pronouncement. She told Grace Hill in 1941 that "Epitaph" was her "challenge" to men to thrust out the "bad cell" and that she was expressing "her heartfelt tribute to the magnificence of man."[17] It is the kind of tribute communicated by Tragedy; in fact, Minot concludes:

By continually balancing man's greatness against his weakness, Millay has conjured up a miniature tragedy in which man, the tragic hero, is seen failing because of the fatal flaw within him.[18]

Critics have paid more attention to the panoramic breadth of imagination these sonnets exhibit—Minot (67) comments on their effect of universality—than to their technique, which is generally excellent. Millay set herself difficult patterns; she followed the Petrarchan form in all except sonnets 1 and 6, which have Shakespearean octaves. Sonnets 13–15 open with emphatic inversions, and thus with a more formal tone than most, but all the sonnets are dignified. Occasional personifications, as in Sonnet 16, seem old-fashioned. Sonnet 18 begins with lines appropriately filled with continuants—*l, s, m, n, r*—"Here lies, and none to mourn him but the sea, / That falls incessant on the empty

shore, / Most various Man. . . ." Alliteration and assonance are used
with great skill in both 17 and 18. The diction is often distinguished:
for example, *catholic slime* and *ribald stone.*

Of the several poems allied to "Epitaph" the finest is "The Return."
It also emphasizes the failure of human society, which depletes and
defiles Man, the simple animal son of earth. Nature, mindless source of
countless men and other species, cares nothing for the success or failure
of any species; she can give no special regard to Man,

> Who, marked for failure, dulled by grief,
>   Has traded in his wife and friend
> For this warm ledge, this alder leaf:
>   Comfort that does not comprehend. (*CP,* 272)

Judging by history, Man cannot meet the demands of society, even the
domestic circle or friendship; it is better then that he revert to the
unselfconscious animal life. But earth-comfort is the comfort of death
to man as it is to any other animal.

The poet's disillusionment during the early 1930s[19] shows in "Apos-
trophe to Man (*on reflecting that the world is ready to go to war again*),"
which is a vehement satirical snort. In "My Spirit, Sore from March-
ing," she also reveals her loss of hope for human betterment. The
difficulty of removal from human society comes out, however, in several
poems—best in "On the Wide Heath" and "How Naked, How without a Wall." "On the Wide Heath," with its unusual stanza pattern and
fine rhythmic effects, consists of one long sentence in which "home,"
the initial word in four lines, is emphasized—a "home" as disagreeable
as possible but tolerated—"it being / Too lonely, to be free" (*CP,* 301),
as Millay finally interprets the situation. "How Naked" (*CP,* 311–12)
stresses more the pain of trying to travel independently. Such phrases as
"whispering ditch," "rising chill," "tiny foot," and "helpless shadow"
express vividly on both the literal and the symbolic level the nervousness and fears of the nightfarer and the deadliness of his exposure "when
other men are snug within" their comfortable, orthodox opinions.[20]
The personal lyrics of the volume also show more objective consideration of the poet and her relation to a world in which she has to accept age
and death.

Millay wrote a group of six poems (*CP,* 283–91) in memory of her mother, each with its own form. The finest one is "In the Grave No Flower," which emphasizes the omnipresence of weeds on earth—dock, tare, beggar-ticks, thistles, and many more—"but there no flower." The choked voice of grief is perfectly rendered with abrupt, short, stabbing lines:

> . . . here
> Dandelions,—and the wind
> Will blow them everywhere.
> Save there.
> There
> No flower. (*CP,* 285)

Wine from These Grapes deserved the approval it received from various critics on the grounds of maturity, development, and a tautening of line comparable to the change from earlier to later Yeats.[21]

Flowers of Evil

Millay's preface to *Flowers of Evil* supplies important information for the assessment of the Dillon-Millay translations of Baudelaire. She assumes, first, that the shape of a poem is very significant; consequently, she approves of Dillon's decision to translate each poem in the same meter and form that Baudelaire had used. Thus the majority of the poems in the collection have been translated into hexameters instead of into pentameters, the staple of English poetry. The decision that a poem in translation should have not only the meaning of the original but also the same look and something of the same sound accounts for the fact that the translators had to elaborate many of Baudelaire's lines, just as Baudelaire himself, translating the eight-syllable lines of Longfellow's *Hiawatha* into alexandrines, was forced to elaborate.[22]

Translations, like grammars, are always leaky; and, on the basis of their principles, considerable freedom must be conceded Millay and Dillon. Millay acknowledged that they found they got closer to their desired effects by introducing one or two extra syllables into a hexameter line, that they were bitterly aware of necessary losses in translation, that some of the poems were very freely rendered, and that translation often entails differences in terms of concrete detail and generality. In fact, Millay's discussion of these poems, "shipwrecked into English and fitted out with borrowed clothes," anticipated most of the objections raised by reviewers.[23]

The Dillon-Millay *Flowers of Evil* contains seventy-two poems, nearly half of Baudelaire's published poetry. Thirty-six were translated by Millay, thirty-five by Dillon, and one, "The Fleece" *(La Chevelure)*, by both. "The Fleece," like many of the others, illustrates the unevenness of the translations when they are judged in terms of precision and economy. Stanzas 1 and 3 are not very accurate: the figure is altered in line 6: *Je la veux agiter dans l'air comme une mouchoir!* becomes "I long to rake it in my fingers, tress by tress!" And lines 11–12 introduce extra abstract terms. But stanzas 2, 4, and 5 are well done and parts of stanzas 6 and 7, although "glittering with many a star" (line 31) and "every stone that gleams" (line 37), are commonplaces that dilute the poetry; "sycamored" (line 38) seems brought in only for the rhyme.

Millay translated several of Baudelaire's most substantial poems: *Rêve Parisien, L'Invitation au Voyage, Les Litanies de Satan, Les Sept Vieillards, Une Martyre, Le Voyage,* and *Bénédiction.* Her rendering of *Bénédiction* has extra phrases: line 1, "On a certain day"; line 4, "in scorn"; line 12, "reeking of stale lust." Yet much of the poem is good—for example, stanza 6:

> *Pourtant, sous la tutelle invisible d'un Ange,*
> *L'Enfant déshérité s'enivre de soleil,*
> *Et dans tout ce qu'il boit et dans tout ce qu'il mange*
> *Retrouve l'ambroisie et le nectar vermeil,*

which Millay translates:

> Meantime, above the child an unseen angel beats
> His wings, and the poor waif runs laughing in the sun;
> And everything he drinks and everything he eats
> Are nectar and ambrosia to this hapless one. (261)

Line 3 is precise; and of the rest one can complain only that "runs laughing" scarcely does justice to *s'enivre* and that the vivid *vermeil* is omitted.

"Travel" (*Le Voyage*) is rather wordy, yet often suggests the quality of the original. The next-to-last stanza, however, with the famous address to *Mort, vieux capitaine* is unsatisfactory: *O Mort, vieux capitaine, il est temps! levons l'ancre! / Ce pays nous ennuie, ô Mort! Appareillons!* becomes "Oh Death, old captain, hoist the anchor! Come, cast off! / We've seen this country, Death! We're sick of it! Let's go!" (245). Even allowing utmost freedom to the translator, one must boggle at this rendering as too undignified, too modern.[24]

"Invitation to the Voyage" makes an advantage of short curling and sweeping run-on lines (Millay's run-on lines are sometimes a drawback in the rendering of Baudelaire's hexameters). The refrain, "There, restraint and order bless / Luxury and voluptuousness," is a fairly good substitute for *Là, tout n'est qu'ordre et beauté, / Luxe, calme et volupté.* In general, the stanzas are well rendered although the last half of stanza 3 loses something of Baudelaire's effect because of a different order of details and the weakly general "all things in sight" (77).

Millay does best with the poems of Baudelaire which express sordid qualities of Parisian life, to which he was especially sensitive, and the *spleen* they induced. Her translation of *Une Martyre* ("Murdered Woman") is very good, particularly the last stanza:

> In vain your lover roves the world; the thought of you
> Troubles each chamber where he lies:
> Even as you are true to him, he will be true
> To you, no doubt, until he dies. (207)

The end of "Parisian Dream" is handled very well (57–59), and "Dawn" (*Le Crépuscule du Matin*) conveys accurately the seedy, dismal, O-God-not-again impression of *le sombre Paris* (169–71). Some of the sonnets are excellently done also, such as *Spleen I, Brumes et Pluies* ("Mists and Rains"), and *La Cloche Fêlée* ("The Cracked Bell").

Millay the ironist was a congenial translator of *L'Imprévu* ("The Unforeseen"); in it, as in *Bien Loin d'Ici* ("Ever So Far from Here"), she produces very well the tone of cutting ironical disgust, the sarcastic rebuke of Baudelaire's rasped, fastidious exasperation. The theme of hastening Time, which obsessed Baudelaire, was also congenial to Millay; her translation of *L'Horloge* is one of her best. If many of Millay's translations have in them more of Millay than of Baudelaire, the reader should not be surprised. Nevertheless, many of them are more accurate than other translations of Baudelaire.

Conversation at Midnight

Millay counseled readers to consider *Conversation at Midnight* in terms of a play rather than of a narrative poem (Foreword, viii). It is not, however, a play in the usual sense; it is a dialogue among seven men of differing backgrounds and beliefs who meet for an evening of conversation and drinking—literally, for a symposium. From its Platonic beginnings the dialogue form has had a great history. It flourished during the Renaissance, being used for discussions of all kinds of subjects: love, ethics, religious debates, witchcraft, and dramatic poesy. Though used less in modern literature, the form is still not dead.

John Peale Bishop said that Millay's characters are only "dramatized points-of-view" and that her work would lack the staying power of a dialogue like *The Courtier* in which the characters were real, being Castiglione's friends.[25] Granted that *Conversation* shows only a modicum of characterization, one might better place it with the "philosophical" novels of Peacock, such as *Headlong Hall,* than with either *The Courtier* or a stiff set-piece like Dickinson's *A Modern Symposium,* as Wilson suggested.[26] Millay's work, like Peacock's, allows people representing current ideologies to explain themselves and attack their companions' crotchets.[27]

Something of Millay's attitude during the time when she was writing *Conversation at Midnight* may be seen in the reports of an interview she gave on 5 December 1934, just after returning from two months of readings in the South, the very day on which the Senate in its sensational arms inquiry was shown what power arms manufacturers had wielded at Geneva in 1925.[28] Millay told reporters she was disillusioned:

"I am disgusted with the hollow talk of disarmament. . . . We put wreaths on the grave of the Unknown Soldier, who's pretty damn well known by now as the symbol of the next war . . . while Japan penetrates China. . . . We will never have peace so long as the interlocking munitions interests of Germany, France, England, control Governmental parties and influential groups . . . as long as people go on manufacturing death and trying to sell it. . . ."

"Do you think, then, that the profit system must be abolished?"

"Yes, I blame the system . . . it goes back to the profit system . . . I should like to live in a world where everybody has a job, leisure for study, leisure to become wiser, more perceptive . . . I am willing to give up everything I possess, everything I ever will have . . . I am willing to live the simplest life . . . to live in a hut, on a loaf a day (Oh, I do know this sounds idiotic!) to achieve it. . . ."

"Do you want Communism?"

"No, no, I do not . . . Communism is repugnant to me . . . I am intensely an individualist . . . I cannot bear to have a thousand well-wishers breathe on my neck. . . ."[29]

Another report of the interview said that she "had hit on a compromise between the inequalities of capitalism and the universal rigors of communism." She did not explain herself in any detail, "but implied that her next book might have something to say about it."[30]

From the start she planned to use a variety of metrical forms. The book is written, therefore, in a mixture of styles, comprising sonnets, some strict, others very free in meter; regularly structured lyrics; free verse; and verse with irregular line lengths and irregularly placed rhymes. The tone varies also: it is frequently colloquial, bantering, or satirical; only occasionally does it rise to dignity and eloquence. Although Millay thought well of *Conversation,* she considered the published version inferior to the one that was burned: "There were many passages which I had to re-invent, and others which I was forced to leave out entirely, so that the result is patchy and jerky."

The characters in the dialogue are chosen for diversity. The extremes of wealth and poverty, age and youth, are represented by Merton, sixty-eight, a wealthy stockbroker, art collector, and lover of poetry, and by Lucas, twenty-five, an advertising writer who had to make a penniless start. The five other men are in their forties. Extremes of political commitment are represented by Merton, a Republican; Carl, a Communist poet; and Pygmalion, a cynic and hedonist disillusioned with politics. Extremes of religious belief are represented by Father Anselmo, a Roman Catholic priest, and Ricardo, an agnostic. John, a painter, has a religious nature but cannot thoroughly believe in anything. Ricardo, the host, is a liberal with a subtle mind. Though touching on many topics, their conversation focuses chiefly on the problem of religious, economic, and political faith. Millay divided the work into four parts, but the division has no significance.

As one first hears them, the men are talking about hunting and dogs, the sort of talk Millay heard at the home of George LaBranche, a neighbor in Austerlitz who was a wealthy stockbroker, pheasant raiser, and champion shot. Merton complains of paying five dollars a week for poor training and poor care of a dog. Carl's first comment is a sneer directed at the wasteful consumption of the wealthy. As one would expect of a Communist, Carl, a constant gadfly, is indignant over such waste; he feels the actuality of poverty and depression much more than the others, who are insulated by their wealth or their type of work. He believes that the depression-emergency must override any unproductive, pleasurable uses of leisure (8).

The conversation lights upon religious faith. Ricardo has suggested that John accept Faith "to frost with sugar the foul pill of Death" (9), but John finds it distasteful to take up with God "when you're an interested party" (11). Anselmo makes an analogy of the senses: probably a future age will lack the senses of smell and taste—and will it not then deny the possibility of there being five senses? The analogy leads to a discussion of human limitations, modern developments, and particularly airplane flight, which leads in turn to criticisms of the contemporary world—its noise and speed, the falsity and effectiveness of its advertising (from Lucas, who writes advertising copy), and its abuses of language. Anselmo regrets the degradation of Latin too, and the association with Church Latin brings the talk back to the topic of Faith. This is a fair example of the method by which Millay conducts the dialogue; although she has it under control, the control is disguised by the spiraling progress of the talk often brought about through associations with subjects introduced by analogy or illustration. Thus the dialogue has a convincing realism.[31]

Ricardo expresses what seems to be a paradox: "It is I who have faith . . ." (26). For he believes in the existence of Mystery beyond his immediate horizon, and he accuses Anselmo of an arrogant anthropomorphism: "You cannot conceive that there might be that of which you cannot conceive; you are arrogant; / You endow all things with human attributes; you do not hesitate / To call the inconceivable 'Father'" (27). Anselmo gives a dignified defense of Faith arrived at by the light of Reason. Then the men discuss the questions: why do men fight? what chance is there for peace? John suggests that nations fight for elbowroom; Ricardo says that they fight for empire because man's largely animal nature includes a fighting instinct: Jesus' doctrine of brotherly love "is not characteristic of the species" (35). Anselmo thinks that there may be hope of development, wars being a kind of fermentation. Carl agrees but believes that this cannot happen under Capitalism: "Only in revolution, only in the audible seething of the crushed masses / Does Man ferment to a purpose, to his proper destiny" (36). Ricardo and John see war as a betrayal of Man's best, as the means of debasement. Pygmalion, however, points out that "there's lots of men that love a fight" (38). War is so exciting that it won't be abandoned. Ricardo sadly philosophizes: "War is man's god; he has but one. / And Peace, but the time it takes the unhorsed warriors to mount and come on" (39). Anselmo gives a priest's answer:

> There is no peace on earth today save the peace in the heart
> At home with God. From that sure habitation
> The heart looks forth upon the sorrows of the savage world
> And pities them, and ministers to them; but is not implicated.

He feels, however, that they cannot comprehend his attitude, and after playing some Bach on Ricardo's piano, he soon leaves.

With Part II, Lucas brings up the topic of love, particularly lost love. All the men join in criticisms of women, expressed in a witty parody of Ogden Nash's style; but the love-discussion mainly aids in characterization: one sees the youth and relative inexperience of Lucas (who has fewer than twenty speeches in the whole poem); the down-to-earth sensualism and cynicism of Pygmalion, already indicated by his remarks on war; and the deeper understanding of Ricardo, who is given two "arias"—"The family circumstance" and "If you lived in the north"—more sympathetic to the cause of women and idealistic love.

In their discussion of economic matters, Carl voices proletarian hopes, likening the dictatorship of the proletariat to a second coming. He identifies himself with workers and their dirt: "I honour the dirt . . . / Because it is the dress my mother wore" (66). He likens the Communists to a group of friends around a campfire which provides light; furthermore, he regards the triumph of communism as inevitable. On the other side, Merton favors tradition, and Carl accuses him of simply not being able to accept change. Carl is, of course, an antitraditionalist: the "Brocaded Past" is a heavy "drag upon the shoulders" (71). Meanwhile, Ricardo regrets the modern Babel tower created by specialization: "this bean-stalk, Science," will not reach to God.

In Part III, the debate on the value of tradition continues, and Carl emphasizes present needs of "the living world!" (75). Merton and Pygmalion reveal themselves further as practical *hommes moyens sensuels* as they discuss salmon fishing and horse breeding, among other matters; and Carl shows that he is something more than a fanatic during the discussion of mushrooms. Ricardo, the subtle-minded individualist, voices another "aria" on individualism and its difficulties ("The mind thrust out of doors,") which recalls some of the lyrics in *Wine from These Grapes* (78–79).

Carl and Merton clash again. Carl insists that there must be a revolution that will put machines to work for men. Ricardo points to the Communist record in Russia where communism has to be imposed by a dictator like Stalin, "the dissenting mouth stopped up with unarguable lead" (88). Merton sees in the Russian situation a dark prospect for culture; but Carl scoffs at conventional American "culture," which means going through gestures considered "correct" or merely collecting things "either old or rare" while sneering at anything beautiful but common. He expresses the best of Communist aspiration in the fine lyric "Beautiful as a dandelion blossom, golden in the green grass, / This life can be" (90). Seeing man as evil, Merton is disillusioned of any such hopes by the "recent altercations / Within the Left"[32] (91). And both Ricardo and Pygmalion reprove Carl for emotionalism, for regarding communism as religion when it is supposed to be science. In Part IV, Ricardo criticizes the lack of distinction under communism; each person is only a cog in an impersonal machine.

Midnight arrives. The company think of differing time zones in Europe. Thus John has a chance to enforce the midnight-theme:

> . . . I fear that in Paris, too,
> It is midnight. Midnight in London; midnight in Madrid.
> The whole round world rolling in darkness, as if it
>   feared an air-raid.
> Not a mortal soul that can see his hand before his face. (97)

This metaphor of darkness—that of fear, ignorance, indecision— bitterly gives point to the title of the volume. Yet, Pygmalion surmises,

Mussolini and Hitler see their way before them. Ricardo speaks vigorously in England's favor. But when Carl challenges them to do something to prevent another war—to fight fascism instead of wringing their hands—they do not take up the challenge.

Carl goes further by accusing Merton (as a capitalist) of having failed and being unfit to rule. This is criticism after the Auden-Spender fashion. Merton retaliates with the charge that Communists enjoy freedom in a democracy which they deny in Russia. Carl's defense is lame; it amounts to assuming that criticism would be out of place under the perfect Soviet government. Carl is confident of Communist victory because of wholeness and undivided effort. Merton counters that these qualities also apply to Hitler, and Ricardo reminds them that "singleness of purpose and direct approach" belonged to many an extinct race "that knew what it wanted and followed its nose" (109). Carl applies the parallel to capitalism—"a prehistoric monster."

Ricardo remains an arch-individualist; he believes in neither God nor communism, and he dislikes the mass of people: "And I would rather stand with my back against an icy, unintelligible void / Than be steamed upon from behind by the honest breaths of many well-wishers" (111). His lot is particularly difficult. Carl taunts him with having no program. Ricardo admits the weakness of the liberal position. Even so, John thinks the liberal view is an "insistent leaven" (113). Carl gloats over the coming victory of communism; but Pygmalion roughly accuses communism of stifling independent thought—communism is the opium of the dissatisfied.

The hour grows late, and Ricardo's party grows louder and rougher. After they come at last to trading insults, Ricardo asserts himself as host and moderator to restrain his guests. They have another drink and soon leave—exhilarated and still friends. Nothing has been settled during the conversation. But during this dialogue the chief opposing political and social philosophies of the dark time of 1937 have been thrown into conflict. The assumptions of each speaker and the things he values most have been made clear. Each one has scored points against his opponents; Millay has kept the balance reasonably even, although her own sympathies are with Ricardo, the Humanist Liberal, the least opinionated and the most reasonable of the disputants.[33]

Few reviewers were enthusiastic about *Conversation at Midnight*. Some felt that Millay, not perceiving that the incendiary hand of

Providence had been at work on Sanibel Island, had mistakenly dredged her memory and salvaged the work. It was too "modernistic," too prosy, too inconclusive. Perhaps, as Patton holds, reviewers generally did not see *Conversation* in the right perspective. It should be ranged, he believes, with the socially conscious, argumentative discussion plays of the 1930s written by Auden, Spender, MacNeice, and MacLeish.[34] Some of the same problems and attitudes appear in *The Dog Beneath the Skin* (1935) and *The Ascent of F 6* (1937) by Auden and Isherwood, MacNeice's satirical extravaganza *Out of the Picture* (1937), and Spender's *Trial of a Judge* (1938). In general, however, these works are far more conventionally theatrical (although of expressionistic type) than *Conversation* is.

MacLeish's *Panic* (1935) has passages that are closer to the tone and spirit of Millay's work—for example, the denunciation of "the Revolution" by the financier McGafferty, which could as well be voiced by Merton or Pygmalion.[35] One may safely say that all these writers, like many others of the trying 1930s, became socially conscious and felt that the socioeconomic problems of the time demanded expression. Millay had earlier, in *Aria da Capo,* addressed herself to a dramatic problem in a special type of verse. She would have enjoyed expressing her penchant for satire, and obviously she became more and more concerned for the world situation. It was not uncharacteristic of her to write *Conversation;* and as a poetic technician, she must have liked working with the various meters she used.

In letters to the author, Witter Bynner praised *Conversation* as a symposium; and Maxwell Anderson its effectiveness as dialogue; he encouraged Millay to write actively for the theater.[36] In fact, given belated production in Los Angeles in November 1961, *Conversation* played successfully for sixteen weeks;[37] a New York production of 1964 closed, however, after four performances. Critics thought the work dated, undramatic, and lacking in effective characterization for the stage.

Although it has some lyric passages, *Conversation* comes mainly from the head and not the heart; it is prevailingly colloquial in style. Those who censure the work because it does not give a decisive message or because it is insufficiently lyrical are regarding it the wrong way. It may be censured, however, for too slack a prosiness at times. Sudden shifts, too, from the loosely fingered lines to sonnets and "arias" take one unbelievably fast from one emotional level to another. Most readers now, nearly fifty years after it was written, will probably find the poem dated. Nevertheless, it is a witty production charged with the spirit of Nancy Boyd.

Huntsman, What Quarry?

Huntsman, What Quarry?, published in May 1939, represents not only work of the previous five years but some going back even as far as 1927. It seems an uneven volume, a less sustained achievement than Millay's other collections, giving the impression that her imagination may have been too much distracted during the 1930s. In subject matter it resembles earlier volumes but with a different mixture. It has a few descriptive poems, a small group of philosophical pieces, another on political-social topics, and a third dealing with love and sex. The largest category is made up of personal poems, often pervaded by regret and a sense of loss.

"English Sparrows" describes the coming of dawn over Washington Square; for once a positive response to New York, it is an agreeably Whitmanesque poem with Millay's customary precision of observation. In the spring of 1934 Millay visited Llewelyn Powys, ill with tuberculosis, in Dorsetshire, and "The Ballad of Chaldon Down," telling of her visit through his words, is largely descriptive, as is "Impression: Fog Off the Coast of Dorset."[38] Other poems reflect life at Steepletop, such as "The Snow Storm" and "The Rabbit," the latter touching on the mystery of wild creatures and of death. The sonnet "Now that the west is washed . . ." (*CP,* 687) relates the beauty of the planet Venus to the situation of a downed airplane pilot.

Among the philosophical pieces the title poem of the volume is the finest. It contrasts the masculine and the feminine—masculine dedication to action and violence, feminine conservatism and tenderness. One may think, with Rosenfeld, that the huntsman symbolizes man's endeavor to attain the Ideal or Truth or the Absolute, "the hot pads / That ever run before" (*CP,* 332). Those who take up that ceaseless, demanding pursuit cannot be deflected by worldly pleasures.[39] Pictorial, economical, and dramatic, the poem is a masterly achievement.

The sonnet "Now let the mouth of wailing for a time" is an ironic challenge to mourners who believe in a Heaven and thus should not grieve: "Grief that is grief and worthy of that word / Is ours alone from whom no hope can be / That the loved eyes look down and understand" (*CP,* 685). However she may have accepted the Christian ethic and felt mystical reverence, Millay remained firmly agnostic.[40] But "Lines Written in Recapitulation" and "This Dusky Faith," although confessions of failure to influence the course of the world, are vigorous assertions of a humanist faith in man. The other side of this coin is shown by the sonnets "Upon this age, that never speaks its mind" and "My earnestness, which might at first offend," the second much more successful than the first, which has a confused mixture of images although it tries to be Wordsworthian.

The defeat of democratic Spain and the appeasement of Germany and its expansion were events that drew Millay's interest. "Say That We Saw Spain Die" is a tribute to democratic Spain as a bull in a bull-ring dying brutally of loss of blood. "From a Town in a State of Siege," a group of five sonnets from a girl's point of view (not reprinted in later collections), is evidently based also on the Spanish War. When Bohemia-Moravia became a German protectorate on 15 March 1939 and Slovakia followed on 16 March, Millay wrote the sonnet "Czecho-Slovakia," one of the best of her political poems.[41] Full of pity, she stresses the harshness of the time, the lack of honor and mercy. "The barking of a fox has bought us all" refers either to Hitler or to Neville Chamberlain. The betrayal-allusion at the end is a satirical triumph: "While Peter warms him in the servants' hall / The thorns are platted and the cock crows twice" (*CP,* 692).

In the first two of "Three Sonnets in Tetrameter" Millay deplores the growing coarseness and vulgarity of the world with its increasing masses. In the third sonnet she expresses sadness over the Sino-Japanese war, which further disappoints her hopes of "A human peace that might endure" (*CP,* 696). Shattering of idealistic hopes is constantly reflected in Millay's poems of the 1930s.

Two lyrics are about disappointed love. "The Princess Recalls Her One Adventure" is a restrained poem in the early-Millay manner which implies a girl's frustration behind the constraints of protocol. Lines 10–17 are especially good. "Short Story," with a poetic melody suggesting folksong, sketches an affair unhappily broken off because an English girl could not adjust to America. In "Pretty Love, I Must Outlive You," Millay again stresses the transiency of love; but with a hint of folktale "Song for Young Lovers in a City" shows sympathy for those who "in a rented bed have met, . . . / Against a background of despair" (*CP*, 328).

A few of the personal poems are attempts at self-analysis. "The Plaid Dress" is an allegory in which she decides that she can never rid herself of her ingrained bad qualities. Although she might have lived a restrained and feelingless life, she asserts in "Fontaine, Je Ne Boirai Pas . . . ," she has lived with passion, and now it is difficult to attain even a little peace. But "I must not die of pity," she writes in Sonnet 139; she must make herself strong in order to perform her proper function as an effective poet. Sonnet 126, "Thou famished grave, I will not fill thee yet," and Sonnet 130, "Be sure my coming was a sharp offense," are typical defiances of death.

"I too beneath your moon, almighty Sex" is also a defiant sonnet asserting that her work is absolutely sincere, "wrought from what I had to build with," coming out of her far from perfect self and including lust "and nights not spent alone" (*CP*, 688). "Menses" is far more original, in part a tribute to Boissevain but also a frank poetic representation of menstruation as a psychological problem in marriage. Its subtitle is "He speaks, but to himself, being aware how it is with her," and it dramatizes how the sympathetic husband tactfully deals with the harsh and unreasonable, but temporary, cantankerousness of the wife. Again Millay condemns her body for interfering with her mind.

Some of the personal poems reflect the affair with George Dillon. "The Fitting" comes out of 1932, when she was having dresses made in Paris and he was there on a Guggenheim fellowship. The poem intimates the passion and seriousness of a love affair without saying anything directly about it and depends on the contrast between the matter-of-fact ignorance of the fitter—"*Ah, que madame a maigri!*"—and the customer's knowledge about the reason for her thinness, the seriousness of which she is not willing to admit even to herself. She makes an excuse: "*C'est la chaleur.*" But her thoughts are with her lover, whose caresses she is contrasting with the rude handling she receives from the shopwomen:

> I stood for a long time so, looking out into the
>   afternoon, thinking of the evening and you. . . .
> While they murmured busily in the distance, turning me,
>   touching my secret body, doing what they were
>   paid to do.[42] (*CP*, 343).

Implied is a contrast with a lover who does not have to be paid for his secret intimacies. "Rendezvous" is about a meeting with a lover in Greenwich Village; no longer young, the woman takes pleasure in the affair but not what she would have had when younger; for the poem ends with: "And I wish I did not feel like your mother" (*CP*, 341).

Apparently "Thanksgiving Dinner" is about the dissolving of the romance of her marriage into routine domesticity; if so, it is a wry celebration of a love which must now feed on "steaming, stolid winter roots" (*CP*, 330).

The most impressive of the love poems is "Theme and Variations," a presentation of a woman involved in an affair with an unworthy man. She recognizes clearly his unworthiness; yet "rolled in the trough of thick desire," she suffers, saddened by the sordidness of the situation. Section IV is particularly Meredithian: the lovers scarcely bother to deceive one another; finally "even the bored, insulted heart" will "break its contract." Other loves made her proud, however difficult they were or inadequate she was; but this one hurts in a special way: "Not that this blow be dealt to *me*: / But by thick hands, and clumsily."

She can wish for the peace of the grave, but what she should do is to have enough strength of will to cut off the affair. At the end, however, she finds herself overly involved, perversely committed to this person who is not "fit subject for heroic song"; she cannot free herself: "That which has quelled me, lives with me, / Accomplice in catastrophe" (*CP*, 355–67).

Notes of regret and mourning run through the volume. Millay's grief over the death of her poet friend is expressed in "To Elinor Wylie," a group of six poems composed in different forms and at different times. It is rather like a suite of music. It moves from an assertion of love, "Song for a Lute," a beautiful lyric in an Elizabethan strain, through reminders of Wylie's beauty and interests to mourning for her loss in mid-career, "Shaken from the bough, and the pure song half-way through" (*CP*, 375).

The finest of the personal poems is the autumnal, regretful but acquiescent "Not So Far as the Forest." With senses less keen, the middle-aged person begins to live in memory more than in the present, neglected for its familiarity:

> Night falls fast.
> Today is in the past.
>
> Blown from the dark hill hither to my door
> Three flakes, then four
> Arrive, then many more.

The approach of age is symbolized by a gradually dying tree; by the death of Love, unheroically stung by gnats in a swamp; and finally by the frustrated flight of a bird with clipped wing:

> Though Time refeather the wing,
> Ankle slip the ring,
> The once-confined thing
> Is never again free. (*CP*, 335–39)

Since Millay so passionately loved freedom and hated restraint, the poem must have come out of real anguish. It expresses her sense of loss—loss of keen response because of dulling familiarity and acceptance of things-as-they-are, and loss of lyric capacity with the years. In essence this poem is her "Intimations Ode," in which she tells how the glory and the dream are gone.

In much of the volume one may see, however, how years have brought the philosophic mind. The poems of *Huntsman, What Quarry?* come from a woman of forty who looks on life with some chagrin and who has learned to express herself, at her best, in language that is crisp, usually contemporary, and non-"literary."

Make Bright the Arrows and The Murder of Lidice

On 23 August 1939, the German-Russian pact was signed. World War II began with the German invasion of Poland on 1 September. When Millay appeared at the *Herald-Tribune* Forum in New York on 24 October, she criticized the atmosphere of neutrality: "As regards war between a Germany whose political philosophy is repugnant to us, and an allied Britain and France whose concepts of civilized living are so closely akin to our own," why should Americans not say they hope Britain and France will win?[43] Thus Millay, consistently anti-Fascist, favored a strong armed position for democratic nations; her common sense told her that pacifism or appeasement would be a dangerous policy for the United States.

From the moment the Germans invaded the Low Countries on 10 May 1940, Millay began writing propaganda verse. At the very moment when disaster fell on the British at Dunkerque "There Are No Islands, Any More" appeared in the *New York Times Magazine,* 2 June 1940—"Lines Written in Passion and in Deep Concern for England, France, and My Own Country." She might have included her husband's country; for both she and Boissevain felt concern about his relatives in Holland; furthermore, the German conquest meant that he had lost all his wealth abroad.

Her propaganda verse was collected in *Make Bright the Arrows; 1940 Notebook.* The subtitle she hoped would indicated that the work was unpolished. Evidently she thought that by rousing the country to arm she would help to keep it out of war. In the title poem she says: "Stock well the quiver / With arrows bright: / The bowman feared / Need never fight" (vi).[44] Although critical readers honored her sincerity, they knew that the book at best was mere journalism—and also, unfortunately, poor propaganda, as Ficke thought it: "being so largely hysterical and vituperative. . . ."[45] Too often Millay fails to exhort and merely wields the lash. The most acceptable pieces are "Memory of England" (written in October 1940 during the terrible bombings of England), in which she could dwell with vivid and loving memory on English experiences she and her mother had had; and some of the sonnets.

On 10 June 1942, the Nazi government announced that the village of Lidice, Czechoslovakia (population 446), had been razed; all the men killed; and the women and children sent to labor camps, in reprisal for the assassination of Reinhard Heydrich, the "protector" of Bohemia and Moravia, known by the Czechs as Heydrich the Hangman. Immediately the Writers' War Board requested of Millay a commemorative poem.

The Murder of Lidice is a ballad set between introductory and closing
hortatory material. Life in Lidice is presented in terms of the cycle of
seasons, of work, of marriage: "First came Spring, with planting and
sowing; / Then came Summer, with haying and hoeing; / Then came
Heydrich the Hangman, the Hun . . ." (7). Karel and Byeta grow up,
become engaged, and are to marry on 10 June 1942. Clairvoyant Byeta
has premonitions that she will never marry, and her father is fearful
after he hears that Heydrich has died. Much is made of the horror of the
Nazi executions, burnings, and butchery. Karel crawls, dying, to
Byeta; and she kills herself rather than become a slave to a German
officer. Millay gives the situation the aspect of legend by reporting that
people say that on 10 June the village is still there, the citizens going
about their customary tasks. At the end she addresses "Careless
America, crooning a tune: / . . . Think a moment: are *we* immune?"
(32).

The ballad style tends to mitigate the triteness of the writing; but it
is not a good poem except in the parts concerning the seasonal activities
of the village. The style is reminiscent of nineteenth-century balladry,
even of Poe's "Annabelle Lee" and Alfred Noyes's "The Highwayman."
The poem is mainly overdone; instead of rising, it falls from emotional
strain.

More interesting than such material written to assignment are the
poems Millay wrote to indicate the spirit in which she thought the war
must be waged and the world reconstructed later. The idealistic "Not to
Be Spattered by His Blood," composed soon after Pearl Harbor was
attacked, expressed her confidence in American victory and her concern
that ethical values might be utterly destroyed in the war. Millay told
Grace King that "we must conquer the forces in our own hearts that
breed hatred and enmity among men."[46] "To the Leaders of the Allied
Nations," published in January 1945, shows Millay's old radical distrust of Establishments and a democratic desire for a radically renovated
world. She demands that the leaders exhibit blueprints for "a new /
World—a decent one this time, a world a man might live in without
shame"; for Americans "at this war's end / Not only hope, but, yes, by
God, intend / To see our dreams come true!"—in contrast to the results
of World War I.

Mine the Harvest and *Collected Poems*

The posthumous volume *Mine the Harvest* is the epitome of Millay's poetry, but it shows a greater reflective cast. The poems fall mainly into three categories. First are poems largely descriptive, showing her responses to life in the places where she lived, especially Steepletop, to which she restricted herself increasingly during her last decade. Second are personal poems expressing her feelings and opinions, and third are poems in which she meditates on the human condition.[47]

Though not primarily a nature poet, Millay convincingly conveys the feel of life intensely experienced in various places. "The American scenes she knows are set down with a truth unsurpassed in American poetry," wrote Cook.[48] In *Mine the Harvest* her accustomed vividness of observation suffered no lessening. "The Strawberry Shrub" is perhaps the finest example of her use of the meticulous, exquisitely exact detail through most precise diction, as in "like musty chocolate" and "clinker-built." The description of the flower in terms of Greece is startlingly apt—"something from the provinces: / A chunky, ruddy, beautiful Boeotian thing!" (*CP*, 455–56). Another brilliant descriptive poem is "New England Spring, 1942." In places Millay conveys the spirit of the season; in others, precise images, as of the tapping of maples, with the sap dripping into pails "through tubes of hollow elder"—the old-fashioned spiles which farmers used to make for themselves—; the birds about the pails; the return of snow. The rush of long lines is nicely balanced by the check and wheel of short ones. The close relates the poem to the theme of unendurable beauty: "And Spring is kind. / Should she come running headlong in a wind-whipped acre / Of daffodil skirts down the mountain into this dark valley we would go blind" (*CP*, 470).

A somewhat similar piece of vivid description is "Look how the bittersweet . . . ," which deals with autumn and shows that the poet profited from reading Hopkins. It indicates with a special sense of immediacy in its third stanza how the might of nature in a short while easily overcomes the works of man, such as the pridefully erected stone wall broken and "bought up by Beauty now" (*CP*, 543). The poem has a becoming sound pattern and excellent trochees for portraying men's efforts in handling heavy rocks. The dramatic "Men Working" (*CP*,

532–34) shows Millay's admiration for the skill of four men who with pikes raise a forty-foot, one-ton pole. "Charming" is her word for the movement of girls about a May-pole; but the movement of these men, in July, is *beautiful*.

The description of the northern jay in "Sky-coloured bird . . ." (*CP*, 538) is so detailed that it seems labored, although every point is exact. Whereas much of her late work is sharp and spare, one may hear in this poem, and occasionally elsewhere (cf. *CP*, 494–96. 535–36), an unusual richness of sound through internal rhymes. Her versification is excellent in "To a Snake," where she expresses mixed feelings about a dying fellow-mortal killed by a dog. The close is climactic: "that red, flickering tongue" (*CP*, 540) suggests the dying fire of life and the snake's defiance to the end. "I woke in the night . . . ," vigorous and colloquial, also has a good verse movement and effectively communicates her response to the onset of a blizzard.

One of Millay's annoyances at Steepletop was the importunities of inquisitive visitors, who wasted her time—"I throw bright time to chickens in an untidy yard," she writes in "Cave Canem" (*CP*, 499). She takes up this theme again in the sonnet "What chores these churls do put upon the great" (*CP*, 727). In spite of the rather unfortunate first line, which suggests egotism and an elitism not popular now, lines 6–8 show the decency of the author even though exasperated by "specious hands" trying to get "some thinly-needed / Answer or autograph." Such phrases give the sonnet an almost Miltonic tone, and the final couplet skillfully conveys the *decrescendo* of broken and ebbing thought. Because of such exasperations she appreciated the purity and Nirvana-like tranquillity of her island, as she tells of it in the partially descriptive "Ragged Island"—in which there are excellent examples of that "fascinating tension of timing" that Millay achieved in much of her latest poetry.[49]

The personal poems are of several kinds: first, on the intensity of her experiences and her ecstasy while undergoing them; second, on writing of poetry; third, on love; fourth, on dreams; fifth, on her grief and pain.

Millay views her experiences of beauty almost as sexual passion—"the unendurable embrace" (*CP*, 531). In "This / Is mine, and I can hold it" (*CP*, 448) she tells of her ecstasy listening to a thrush singing: ". . . I may be shattered / Like a vessel too thin / For certain vibrations." And in "The sea at sunset can reflect" she describes the beauty of the sea, the stars, and the Northern Lights—the last experience, paradoxically, an ordeal. These poems are not far in spirit from "God's World," but the verse has greater intellectual control. "How did I bear it . . ." (*CP,* 530) contrasts the intense sense impressions of childhood with her response to the loveliness she encounters as a mature woman ". . . grown up and encased / In the armour of custom"—even prudently wearing rubbers. The experience is still almost overwhelming.

The first two sonnets of the collection also represent a looking back on intense experience—in "Those hours when happy hours were my estate,—" as on the gardens of an estate now "looked at through an iron gate." It cannot be revisited, but "I smell the flower, though vacuum-still the air; / I feel its texture, though the gate is fast" (*CP,* 719). In the following sonnet Millay insists that for her, reality has been as splendid as her dreams; her experiences of "music, and painting, poetry, love, and grief" have been almost unbearably intense (*CP,* 720).

One of her ecstasies, too, had been reading. How real the world of fiction was to her as a child she brings out in "To whom the house of Montagu."[50] This sweetly whimsical piece is in tetrameter, largely in run-on couplets, and contains but one sentence, fifty-one lines long. She smiles at herself as a girl, thinking how close and intimate and indiscriminately mingled in her imagination were the people and settings of *Romeo and Juliet, Don Quixote,* the Troy story, *Venus and Adonis, Hero and Leander,* and the world of classical mythology. In her world ". . . naked long Leander swam / The Thames, the Avon and the Cam," and "any man in any wood"

>   . . . could ride
> A horse he never need bestride—
> For such a child, that distant time
> Was close as apple-trees to climb,
> And apples crashed among the trees
> Half Baldwin, half Hesperides. (*CP,* 447)

In two sonnets she comments on her writing of propaganda verse: "To hold secure the province of Pure Art" and "And if I die, because that part of me" (*CP,* 723–24). They represent her considered opinion that she did well to write her impure verse trying to defend what she believed in. Although rather Wordsworthian, they are stiff and self-conscious. More interesting is "I will put Chaos into fourteen lines" (*CP*, 728), Millay's comment on the process of creating poetry. It is based on the folk-motif of the shape-changer. Chaos is to be held "in the strict confines / Of this sweet Order," the order of the sonnet. The sestet speaks of the hours and the years of the poet's struggle against Chaos, finally victorious. "Something simple not yet understood" is a telling phrase for the amorphous material of a poem which the poet at last shapes and controls.

Among the love poems, "How innocent we lie . . ." (*CP*, 473) is a naughty, defiant piece derisive of respectability. The connotations of *moon* and "cool conniving earth" bolster assertions that sincere stolen love is better than that of "licensed folk." "Armenonville," a sharp vignette with much effective metrical variation, is a reminiscence from Millay's Paris days of a meal in the Bois de Boulogne with a lover. He brought out her shyness by watching her, and she instinctively protected herself by shutting her mind while watching "a small creature" (*CP*, 476). Very different are "Here in a Rocky Cup" and "Truck-Garden Market-Day." The former draws a parallel between rock split by an oak and a woman's heart split by "the seed of love's imperial tree" (*CP*, 471) for which she will willingly "be myself no more at all." In "Market-Day" there is no question of a heroic love, but a farm wife confesses "How small a part of myself I keep" (*CP*, 547) because her concern for her husband overcomes her sense of selfhood.

Mine the Harvest contains a few poems apparently based on dreams. The mysterious "Dream of Saba" recounts the coming of a hurricane upon a ship in the Leeward Islands. The danger of shipwreck is vividly described, and then the miraculous lifting of the ship by a wave into the crater of an extinct volcano. "When the tree-sparrows . . ." is about a dream involving danger to a loved person which made her weep. In "Some Things Are Dark" Nightmare speaks, emphasizing its blackness, compared to which nothing can seem dark.

For strength to endure her griefs she wished that she had been bequeathed "the courage that my mother had" (*CP*, 459)—"That courage like a rock, which she / Has no more need of, and I have." This chiseled lyric with the firmness of Latin epigram is a fine tribute to New

England strength of character. Other poems dwell on her own experience in suffering griefs. The sonnet "Now sits the autumn cricket in the grass" associates the changing of happiness into grief for someone "who died on Michaelmas" with the changing of summer into autumn. After the mention of things that have disappeared with autumn—aconite, roses, swallows, phlox, and asters—the last line, "Nor can my laughter anywhere be found" (*CP,* 733), comes as the perfect summation of one of Millay's finest Petrarchan sonnets. The free-verse piece "At least, my dear" (*CP,* 436) tells something of her thoughts about her husband after his death. She is like a shepherd trying to collect her thoughts like sheep; they are "cropping the mind-bane," memories of deeds that caused him pain. At least he was spared the pain of seeing her die and living thereafter: "The most I ever did for you was to outlive you. / But that is much."

In the sonnet "Felicity of Grief!" the challenge of grief is like a glove, once light and easy to ignore; but to the sufferer it becomes weighty. Thus grief brings felicity in the thought that it could not be so heavy if the loss had not been so great: "Think—of how great a thing were you bereft / That it should weigh so now!—and you knew / Always, its awkward contours, and its heft" (*CP,* 737). Both this poem and the rather involved sonnet "Grief that is grief and properly so hight" lack line seven in the octave.

Millay told Elizabeth Breuer in 1931: "I am a very concentrated person as an artist. I can't take anything lightly. . . . The nervous intensity attendant on writing poetry . . . exhausts me, and I suffer constantly from a headache."[51] Headache is the subject of "And must I then, indeed, Pain, live with you," a stoical-sardonic sonnet in which the poet sees Pain as a parasitical partner in her whole life; but at least it is an evidence of being alive, although it has harmed her. Understatement is usual in these sonnets, as in the final couplet: "You will die with me: but I shall, at best, / Forgive you with restraint, for deeds like these" (*CP,* 734). The sonnet "If I die solvent . . ." suggests a reason for continuing to bear the pains of life—the obligations of her poetic power. Life is a "dark wood," the *selva oscura* of Dante, in which, assailed by wolves (of pain and illness?), she fears that for survival she may have to throw them everything she values. If not, " 'Twill be that in my honoured hands I bear / . . . An earthen grail, a humble vessel filled / To its low brim with water from that brink / Where Shakes-peare, Keats and Chaucer learned to drink" (*CP*, 735).

One of the most noteworthy poems on the human condition is "This should be simple." If one had God-like power, it should be simple—starting fresh and creating from nothing—to bring about a world "at least as beautiful and brave / And terrified and sorrowful as ours" (*CP*, 461). How much greater an achievement would be the creating, now, of good out of accumulated evil—the evil that pervades every part of men's lives. Millay regrets that man has never rightly come to flower, and she indignantly points out many human deficiencies. Efficient persons, accepting evil, can manipulate this world; those devoted to the ideal are hurt and baffled: "Evil alone has oil for every wheel" (*CP*, 465). In spite of disappointments and difficulties, however, she still retains some hope that the world will be improved: we are not up to the task, but future generations may accomplish it: ". . . in some way, yet, we may contrive / To build our world; if not this year, next year" (*CP*, 467). Her romanticism does not include the conviction that man or the world is naturally good; it is, rather, in a vision of future improvement that her romanticism consists.

At times man's evil obscures the vision, as in the sonnet "Read history: so learn your place in Time" (*CP*, 730). She regards history as a repetitive cycle of wars; and, in the twentieth century, warfare has simply been extended through invention and made more efficient. The cycle will continue until men at last root out war. A similar distrust of modern cleverness and intellect appears in "We have gone too far" (*CP*, 427).

"The Animal Ball" (*CP*, 430) satirically stresses the difficulty of man's surmounting his animal inheritance. He tries to disguise himself as a human being, but "The reek of the leopard and the stink of the inky cat / Striped handsomely with white, are in the concert hall. . . ." The sonnet "Read history: thus learn how small a space" (*CP*, 731) places man among hunting beasts in a world of struggle and death where he must protect his little space. Man deserves a special tribute, however; for he is the only animal that knows he must die. And, in the face of that knowledge, he accomplishes everything he does—things to be mar-veled at: "But what a shining animal is man, / Who knows, when pain subsides, that is not that, / For worse than that must follow—yet can write / Music; can laugh; play tennis; even plan." Once more Millay's admiration for human capacities comes out, as it did in "Epitaph for the Race of Man."

In an even finer sonnet, "Tranquility at length, when autumn comes," Millay symbolizes the coming of old age through the arrival of autumn. Summer was a time of action: "to broaden, raise, / proceed, proclaim, establish"; but autumn will allow the mind to be free "One moment, to compute, refute, amass, / Catalogue, question, contemplate, and see . . ." (*CP,* 721).

For the human condition freedom and courage are the essentials. Millay's great affirmation of freedom is "Not for a Nation." Can man as a species survive? Will not lizards, sharks, and cutworms outlive him? Here again is the theme of "Epitaph for the Race of Man"—man, who has weakened himself by nationalistic suspicions, hatreds, and wars. Millay rejects loyalty to divisive principles like nationalism:

Not for the flag
Of any land because myself was born there
Will I give up my life.
But I will love that land where man is free,
And that will I defend.
"To the end?" you ask, "To the end?"—Naturally, to the end. (*CP,* 553–54)

She shows how dearly she appreciates the life of America, familiar and secure; but she treasures most the ideal of human freedom held up by the founders of the United States. They may have been "Men with more courage, men more unselfish, more intent / Than we, upon their dreams, upon their dream of Freedom,—Freedom not alone / For oneself, but for all, wherever the word is known . . ." (*CP,* 557). The poem is another challenge to the greatness of man and, specifically, of Americans. Here, Millay has the last word in her long lovers' quarrel with America.

The poet sometimes used Christian symbols to convey man's sense of sin and need for repentance and hope (cf. "Christmas Canticle," *CP,* 425–26), but her religious attitudes were those of an agnostic concerning the immortality of the soul—according to Grace King, her "mature opinion concerning the Ultimate."[52] In "The Agnostic" Millay describes the situation of an agnostic with very effective images: first, faith is a clearing in a forest—". . . a clearing sunned so bright / He cups his eyeballs from its light" (*CP,* 492); then it is the white light that he can never see, although he is aware of all the colors of the spectrum—"But light evades him: still he stands / With rainbows streaming through his hands." With all his uncertainties, the agnostic is reverent. His attitude is that of John in *Conversation at Midnight*; he would not be a hypocrite and betray his "own heart, which bids him, 'Praise!'" Millay felt, like Tennyson, that "There lives more faith in honest doubt, / Believe me, than in half the creeds." But, like many agnostics, Millay honored the Christian ethic and the imperishable influence of Jesus, as may be seen in "Jesus to His Disciples" (*CP,* 502). Perhaps Humanistic Stoicism, might describe Millay's attitude best. A Stoic temper is implied in many of her poems, especially those in which she speaks of enduring pain and loss.

Mine the Harvest and *Collected Poems* close with a sonnet once part of "Epitaph for the Race of Man"—"What rider spurs him from the darkening east." She projected her imagination into the past as well as the future. The "little bell without a tongue" is flung by the horseman who shouts "Greetings from Nineveh!"; and it reminds man of his ties with the past and his likeness to ancient kingdoms long gone down. The implications of the sonnet were as clear to the poet in the 1920s as when she died five years after the bombing of Hiroshima.

Whether in long rippling lines or in tetrameters, Millay's poetry in *Mine the Harvest* is mainly simple and controlled, not artificial or contrived. It conveys the flavor of living in a world of wonders past or present, the endurance of griefs amid the world's evils. Many of the twenty sonnets in the book (only three in the Shakespearean mode) are as good as any that Millay ever wrote. Packed and rather more intellectualized than most earlier ones, they seem on that account somewhat angular. One is impressed by the thoughtful quality of the volume: it has a "sober coloring" that comes from maturity and the intensely serious regard the poet cast upon life in her later years.

Chapter Six
"A Dream That Wanders Wide and Late"

While Millay was growing up, the Woman Movement was spreading and gathering more and more force. In 1909, the year Vincent graduated from high school, Ellen Key, a Swedish feminist, was writing that young men and women students felt "a friendly comradeship" as they enjoyed folk-dancing, sports, and conversation together; and although she acknowledged that antagonism existed between men and women and that mediocre men were irritated "at the increasing ability of women," she felt that by exercising their strength in gaining a livelihood, women had opportunity to develop complete personality.[1] Even in the 1890s Havelock Ellis had explained that the economic and industrial revolution took women from the home and put men and women to work side by side; the movement for equality begun on the labor level was continuing in educational and political spheres. He concluded that all "discussion regarding the 'alleged inferiority of women'" is "absolutely futile and foolish."[2] Lester F. Ward in his *Pure Sociology* of 1903 had shown that woman's "inferiority" was the result of past subjection, and in 1912 Scott and Nellie Nearing were insisting that a woman is an individual in her own right. The American woman "stands at the parting of the ways. The old world of subjection and dependence lies behind her; before her opens the new world of individual development and achievement."[3]

This "new woman" who left home for steady work in a factory, an office, or some other area of society that offered a career, had clearly emerged before World War I. The 1910 Census Report showed more working women in the United States than ever before and more women who were going to college; in fact, 10 percent of the Ph.D. degrees from American universities in 1910 went to women, and in 1920 they received 15.1 percent of such degrees—a figure not matched since.[4]

These sociological facts were quickly reflected in women's organizations with feminist purposes. Henrietta Rodman, one of the robust, outspoken Village figures, organized the Feminist Alliance in 1914; the members stated that "Feminism is a movement, which demands the removal of all social, political, economic, and other discriminations which are based upon sex, and the award of all rights and duties in all fields on the basis of individual capacity alone."[5] Agitation for Woman Suffrage had been going on since before the Civil War, and from 1913, when twelve states had permitted women to vote, suffragists' pressure for passage of a Woman Suffrage Amendment became progressively stronger.

Broader activities of women and changing attitudes of women and ways of regarding women were connected with the growth of cities and of industries throughout the country. But even in the small towns of Maine a woman like Cora Millay did not hesitate to obtain a divorce as early as 1900 and do nursing to support herself and her three children. So from the time she was eight Vincent Millay had in her mother a constant example of female independence and self-reliance. As she finished high school she also had an example of male jealousy when the boys of her class voted against her as class poet. After high school Vincent found herself in the position of countless girls—not envisioning a career although wishing to be a poet, working at stenographic jobs, perhaps hoping, and certainly expecting some day, to be married, although perhaps, because of her parents' experience, more skeptical over the permanence of love and marriage than most girls would likely be. It seems probable that with the constant encouragement to read in that household, she would have become at least somewhat aware of the Woman Movement.

But of course going away to college at the age of twenty-one—a time when many young women were married, with the responsibilities of a home and children—propelled her into the current of advanced ideas. And she took with her to Vassar the sense of achievement and the fame that "Renascence" had brought her. Vassar, too, reflected the new concepts regarding womanhood and woman's place. President Mac-Cracken called the 1890–1915 era at Vassar the period of the crusader.[6] A Socialist Club and a Suffrage Club were founded there in 1915.[7] Inez Milholland was not only a lawyer and a suffragette but a partisan in the women's labor movement. The Pageant of Athena presented in 1915 was a demonstration of "women's intellectual advancement," and Vincent's play *The Wall of Dominoes,* published in the *Vassar Miscellany Monthly,* May 1917, indicates her awareness of the problems faced by a bachelor girl in New York.

It is evident from her letters that Millay felt a sisterly solidarity with women. As Margaret Widdemer attested, "Edna Millay may have been temperamental, but she was never a woman who didn't want to bother with women's friendship. She had a great many women who were her devoted friends. . . . She was a loyal friend."[8] In 1922 Millay wrote to Edmund Wilson that she had seen "a great deal of Anna Wickham" while in Paris during that spring, and had found her interesting, brilliant, and thrilling. "I like her tremendously." Millay knew Wickham's feminist poetry, which sprang from the tension between "modernity and maternity," for she was a "woman struggling between dreams and domesticity," as Louis Untermeyer wrote.[9] It seems likely that Crystal Eastman, sister of Max Eastman, ardent feminist, militant suffragist, and leader of the Woman's Peace party in New York State, influenced Millay in the direction of feminism and pacifism during the Village years.

Millay was in the first generation of emancipated American women—"an embattled generation" which believed that "'advanced' women should complete their professional training and start careers before marrying at all."[10] As for marriage, after Vassar and the success of her early poetry, she was determined to have a career as a poet; and so, in spite of the assiduous attentions of marriageable men in New York and the attraction that they held for her, she resisted marriage. It seems likely that the ending of Floyd Dell's story "The Kitten and the Masterpiece" is based on his relation with Millay; the heroine refuses the proposal of the hero although she is in love with him: ". . . I don't want to be your wife. I don't want to be anybody's wife. I want to write poetry. . . . That must come first always."[11] On the other hand, various references in her letters, especially as she nears thirty, indicate that she would like to be married and is not reconciled to being an old maid.

Meanwhile, living in New York and in large European cities, Millay shared the urban anonymity that promoted women's freedom: having one's own apartment, smoking cigarettes, drinking cocktails, driving cars, indulging in wild parties, jazz dancing, petting, and sexual freedom generally. All this individual independence she was able to take for granted, particularly after going to Greenwich Village. Floyd Dell, although he gradually became more traditional in his views, was an ardent believer in these new freedoms and in the comradeship of men and women. As a Socialist he favored the Woman Movement. The Village feminists favored socialism, reforms that would eliminate discrimination, allow all women to have labor-saving devices of the new technical society, and both "women and men to become whole human beings who might develop their full potential."[12]

Dell wrote that Millay "was very much a revolutionary in all her sympathies, and a whole-hearted Feminist." He once gave her one of the bronze buttons awarded to women who were arrested for militant suffrage activities, and with tears in her eyes she said, "I would rather have the right to wear this than anything I can think of."[13] Militant suffragists had been picketing the White House since 10 January 1917; but although Millay was a member of Alice Paul's National Woman's party, which pressed zealously for women's suffrage and, after the Nineteenth Amendment was passed, for an Equal Rights Amendment, Millay did not march or demonstrate. Having found her identity as a poet and being certain of her feminist values, she was more concerned to assert her individuality, her right to have a career, unfettered by husband or children, and to do whatever she pleased, unobstructed by outworn conventions and traditional taboos. In her writing and in her life she represented what is "generally spoken of as the revolution in morals of the 1920's" but "is more accurately a revolution in the position of women."[14] Thus, *A Few Figs from Thistles* and other "daring" poems boldly voiced convictions about women and their equality with men that were close to the heart of Greenwich Village.

In Village fiction women scoffed at men for believing in "the mystery and beauty of love and the ethereal qualities of women"; in contrast to the male sentimentalists, the women "talked hardheadedly of the transitory features of life and love."[15] This hardheaded attitude is expressed in such sonnets of Millay's as "I shall forget you presently, my dear," and "Only until this cigarette is ended" (*CP,* 571, 575) as well as in "Thursday" and "To the Not Impossible Him" from *Figs* (*CP,*

129–30), and is implied in "Passer Mortuus Est" (*CP*, 75). Her devotion to her poetic career, which she values more than "the puny fever and frail sweat / Of human love," is strongly asserted in the Pieria sonnet (*CP*, 583). The honesty of the feminist in love affairs, "free from guile," bringing "love in the open hand," and proud that she had not "played you slyly," is expressed in several sonnets of *Fatal Interview* (*CP*, 632, 640, 676). The speaker in that poem is a proudly independent new woman.

But poems in the *Harp-Weaver* volume particularly reveal the contemporary independent woman, for example, the dramatic monologue "The Concert": "No, I will go alone. / I will come back when it's over. / Yes, of course I love you. / No, it will not be long" (*CP*, 186). The speaker, who idealizes music, is explaining to her jealous, possessive lover her preference for attending a concert alone; she can be absorbed in the great art, with which the "you and I" would interfere; the impersonal beauty of music is something greater than the "filigree frame" of their love, and it will make her "a little taller" than before. Though the lover in Sonnet I (*CP*, 584) is "dearer than words on paper"—for a poet, the extreme admission—she anticipates the time when she will again possess the key of her heart. In the next sonnet, the woman, made to eat the "bitter crust" of unrequited love, declares: "But if I suffer, it is my own affair." The situation and the attitude of the intelligent woman who expects to be treated as an equal by men are illustrated by Sonnet 8: "Oh, oh, you will be sorry for that word! / Give back my book and take my kiss instead. / Was it my enemy or my friend I heard, / What a big book for such a little head!" (*CP*, 591). The superior woman's disappointment, her exasperation at being patronized, and her contempt for being thrust (automatically) back into her merely physical role are expressed in "Oh, I shall love you still, and all of that. / I never again shall tell you what I think." She can condescend to conceal herself in conventional femininity but at the sad expense of losing comradely frankness: "I shall be sweet and crafty, soft and sly; / You will not catch me reading any more. . . ." But, finally, she anticipates "some sane day" when "I shall be gone, and you may whistle for me." As we have seen in Chapter 3, Millay's feminism is also manifested from time to time in her short stories.

Several incidents in Millay's life exhibit her adherence to feminist principles. She went to Washington with members of the National

Woman's party for a ceremony honoring early suffragists, and on 18 November 1923—introduced by her friend Doris Stevens, whose book *Jailed for Freedom* (1920) had exposed the illegal and brutal imprisonment of the White House picketers—the "foremost woman poet of America, stirred the audience with a poem she had written for the occasion, and was called back to read it for a second time," *Equal Rights* reported, printing both her sonnet "The Pioneer" and her picture.[16] In her *Collected Sonnets* she retitled the poem "To Inez Milholland"—a gracious tribute by Eugen Boissevain's second wife to his first: "I, that was proud and valiant, am no more;— / Save as a dream that wanders wide and late . . ." (*CP*, 627). More significant in 1923 was the call to further action: "Only my standard on a taken hill / Can cheat the mildew. . . ." Since Millay was listed (19 April 1924) as an associate editor of *Equal Rights,* she certainly approved of the drive for an Equal Rights Amendment, although many women, especially social workers, felt that the Woman's party was only for business and professional women because women workers on wages needed protective legislation.[17]

Probably mixed feminism and Bohemianism caused Millay on 18 April 1927 to send Elinor Wylie an expostulation to be forwarded to the League of American Penwomen. She was protesting their "recent gross and shocking insolence to one of the most distinguished writers of our time":

It is not in the power of an organization which has insulted Elinor Wylie, to honour me.

And indeed I should find it unbecoming on my part, to sit as Guest of Honour in a gathering of writers, where honour is tendered not so much for the excellence of one's literary accomplishment as for the circumspection of one's personal life.

Believe me, if the eminent object of your pusillanimous attack has not directed her movements in conformity with your timid philosophies, no more have I mine. I too am eligible for your disesteem. Strike me too from your lists. . . .

Millay's devastatingly sharp letter was consistent with her scorn for respectability, more especially when it interfered with judgments of literary merit.

When the Boissevains visited the Fickes in New Mexico in the fall of 1926, and after the proofs of *The King's Henchman* had been read, Vincent and Gladys Brown Ficke went from Santa Fe to Zuni, expecting Eugen to join them two days later. Registering as Edna St. Vincent Millay, the poet took a hotel room with Gladys but asked the clerk to reserve a room for Mrs. Ficke, as Mr. Eugen Boissevain was coming to be with her. The clerk refused: hotel policy did not permit such an arrangement. Finally she told him Boissevain was her husband— "Don't you know famous women always use their own names?"[18] Evidently her fame had not extended to the Zuni pueblo; evidently, too, Eugen was more likely to joke over being "Mr. Millay" than she was to change her name.[19]

Millay was fortunate to marry a man who believed in women's rights and was, from the first, willing to subordinate himself to her career. Thus she never had to undergo the lacerating struggle that so many women have had to endure even during the last two decades in order to gain recognition from men of the authenticity and rightfulness of their aspirations to have careers, to achieve lives of their own, or even to emerge from thoughtlessly assumed domesticity.

But even a woman of her fame was not exempt from a slight which she felt as a humiliation because she was a woman. In a letter of 14 June 1937, her feminist principles flashed out as she protested to the Secretary of New York University over not being included among the male recipients of honorary degrees at a dinner given by Chancellor Harry Woodburn Chase.

On an occasion, then, on which I shall be present solely for reasons of scholarship, I am, solely for reasons of sex, to be excluded from the company and the conversation of my fellow-doctors.

Mrs. Chase was including her at a dinner for ladies only.

[But] Mrs. Chase should be the last, I think, to be offended by my attitude. I register this objection not for myself personally, but for all women. . . .

I beg of you, and of the eminent Council whose representative you are, that I may be the last woman so honoured, to be required to swallow from the very cup of this honour, the gall of this humiliation.

Chase had been a psychologist, but his specialty was obviously not the psychology of the new woman. Since for two decades women had not been excluded from clubs and meetings once for men only, Millay's exclusion from the chancellor's dinner—in cosmopolitan New York—must have seemed in 1937 like the action of moss-backed fuddy-duddies.

Millay was a person of great integrity; in any matter of principle she was willing to stand up and be counted. She did not make a career of promoting feminism; but throughout her life she adhered to feminist principles and repeatedly spoke out for the right of women to be judged on their merits as human beings and to be treated as human beings and not as members of an inferior group. If she had been born thirty-five or forty years later, she would certainly have helped women of the present generation in their fight for women's liberation. She long ago anticipated them in steadfast support of the feminist cause: "Take up the song; forget the epitaph" (*CP*, 627).

Chapter Seven
"The Thumbers of the Record"

Criticism of Millay's poetry swung from almost unanimous praise during her early career to extreme neglect and disparagement after her death. A *Wunderkind* of 1912, Millay was in high favor all through the 1920s. She was regarded as a leading American lyric poet and was thought particularly representative of the younger women of the day with their determination to be free of shackling conventions. *A Few Figs from Thistles* received some critical disapproval,[1] but in 1927 Edward Davison placed her next to Frost and Robinson in America, praising her fervor and control while deprecating her tendencies to fever and exaggeration. Rather troubled by her outspokenness, he thought it possible, however, that ultimately her breaking through traditional reticence would be considered a virtue.[2] Among her works "Renascence," *Aria da Capo,* and many sonnets, especially "Euclid alone," received the most consistent approval.

With the appearance of the Sacco-Vanzetti poems in *The Buck in the Snow,* readers began to wonder whether Millay was decisively turning to poetry less subjective, more philosophical and filled with social consciousness. Some critics thought these poems might be portents of a new Millay.[3] Her next volume, *Fatal Interview,* showed her still subjective, however, and still preoccupied with the theme of love. The year of its publication, 1931, saw numerous appraisals of her work, some stressing its traditional quality. McInnis thought she did well not to try to meet public demands for novelty in expression.[4] So did Lewisohn, who in 1932 praised the elemental and timeless in her poetry: she had "not been put to the sterile shifts of mere innovation and experiment. . . ."[5] Allen Tate found her a distinguished poet on a par with Byron and Tennyson, primarily a writer of sensibility who used the vocabulary of nineteenth-century poetry to convey twentieth-century emotion; she brought that language back to life by employing it as her personal idiom: "she has been from the beginning the one poet of our time who has successfully stood athwart two ages. . . ."[6]

As the 1930s continued, Millay received less praise. Some thought her work repetitious; her vocabulary was said to be "literary" or "bookish"; the question was raised whether she could become "mature." Current poetic vogues were making her directness seem old-fashioned. As early as 1935 Edmund Wilson commented on the cycle of praise-disparagement that Millay had been put through—as had numerous contemporaries.[7] *Conversation at Midnight* was widely regarded as a mistake; it was too unlyrical and too different from Millay's usual mode to produce much satisfaction. For all the general sympathy with her aims, the propaganda writings of 1939–41 dismayed many readers, and, after the publication of *Collected Sonnets* (1941) and *Collected Lyrics* (1943), critics lost interest in Millay.

In Minot's opinion, "her reputation has suffered because of matters which have little or nothing to do with the quality of most of her poetry."[8] Her reputation became the victim of a gradual alteration of taste brought about by the influence of the "New Critics" with their anti-Romantic doctrines; the promulgation of these doctrines in the textbooks of Cleanth Brooks and Robert Penn Warren; and especially the domination of the poetic movement called "Modernism" and represented by such writers as Pound, Eliot, W. C. Williams, Tate, and Cummings. They believed (most of them with doctrinaire fierceness) that poets must break away from the past and create new, "modern" modes of expression. As early as 1909, T. E. Hulme, a guru of the movement, declared that the new poetry was not to be chanted; "it appeals to the eye rather than to the ear. . . . It builds up a plastic image which it hands over to the reader, whereas the old art endeavored to influence him physically by the hypnotic effect of rhythm."[9] Modernists generally felt that poets should use the spoken language; poetry "should sound almost like talk."[10] Laying upon the poet the charge of adopting the role of intimate conversationalist, no longer that of seer, prophet, bard, singer, or even reciter, was one of the decisive ways in which modernists drew a line between old and new. W. H. Auden went so far as to write: "The characteristic style of 'Modern' poetry is an intimate tone of voice, the speech of one person addressing one person, not a large audience; whenever a modern poet raises his voice he sounds phony."[11]

Other planks in the modernist platform were more in keeping with poetic tradition—that poetry should be concrete, realistic, and contemporary, that poets should deliberately wish to offend the establishment, and that an organic principle should inform poetry (a justification of free verse).[12] But the principle of discontinuous composition, following a stream-of-consciousness or deliberately abandoning transitions and shifting disconcertingly from one mood or topic to another,[13] was a greater strain on the tolerance of the audience. Over a period of a dozen years this principle was gradually understood, so that Eliot's "The Waste Land" could be digested. But hold-outs like Yvor Winters still protested what he called "the fallacy of imitative form: the attempt to express a state of uncertainty by uncertainty of expression."[14]

Although Millay's poetry is to a large extent in the traditional vein of poetry prophetic, sung, or recited—delivered before an audience, not uttered confidentially to an intimate—it does, in certain respects, fit in with modernist work. Some of it is definitely concrete, realistic, and contemporary—the early New York City and feminist sonnets, for example, much of *Conversation at Midnight* and various lyrics. She often uses twentieth-century colloquial speech. Also Millay, like W. C. Williams, embraced difficult beauty as a proper subject for poetry, and again and again she shows herself to be antiestablishmentarian. On the other hand, she did not abandon traditional forms and she did not make any deliberate effort to use "American" speech or rhythms. She is most definitely antimodernist in her rejection of the "fallacy of imitation." The whole corpus of her work shows this, but in her late sonnet "I will put Chaos into fourteen lines" she explicitly asserts her intention: not for her any attempt to render Chaos in chaotic language. However chaotic the world may seem, the poet must control her concept of that chaos "till he with Order mingles and combines" (*CP,* 728).

Millay and Eliot were not far apart in their judgment of the shortcomings of the modern world, both terribly disillusioned after World War I.[15] Both of them wrote poetry of protest. Sir Herbert Read regarded modern art as "an art of protest—protest against a barbarous civilization that is indifferent to all spiritual and aesthetic values."[16] Millay frequently criticized "this dourest, sorest / Age man's eye has looked upon" (*CP,* 102). Eliot, however, believed that a poet's art "should . . . not express his personality."[17] Being allied to the older, Romantic tradition, Millay differs from Eliot on this point. But the new generation was with Eliot. By 1958 the "whirligig of taste" had so shifted that the distinguished poet John Hall Wheelock said:

> The resistance to feeling directly expressed in the first-person-singular lyric . . . has in our day, been so strong as virtually to eliminate from serious critical consideration the work of such poets as Edna St. Vincent Millay and Sara Teasdale.[18]

Wheelock felt that the literati looked down on poets who wrote love poems.

In terms of ideas the radical Millay was recognized as distinctively modern; she contrasts sharply with reactionaries like Eliot, Pound, and Tate. But poetically Millay was eclectic. She adhered to no poetic "program." She was not doctrinaire about any poetic matters; she felt no need to embrace any program for self-conscious promotion of Imagism (like Pound) or of "modernism" (like Eliot and Tate) or of *American* ways of expression (like Williams). And she was not, like Pound and Eliot, an urban poet and a lightly rooted expatriate with no attachment to the American earth. Although critical of American society and, like them, critical of the age, she remained aware of concrete life in America close to the soil, and she was responsive to all the changes and threats, as well as the beauty and charm, of nature. Much of her poetry is a rural poetry; except in some respects of form, it has more in common with the work of Wordsworth, Vergil, and Housman than with that of the "modernists." She wrote to Ficke in 1912: "The earth passion! I have always had that." And she always retained it.

Another quality somewhat sets her off from the modernists. They spoke much about new rhythms and about colloquial and *American* language. But they were less concerned than Millay with precision of individual word or phrase. Hulme acknowledged that modernist poets were abandoning the attempt to achieve perfect words and form. "Instead of these minute perfections of phrase and words, the tendency will be rather towards the production of a general effect. . . ."[19] Millay continued, as she had done from the start, to strive for that precise word filled with power and surprise which gives so much satisfaction in the poetry of Shakespeare, Milton, Keats, Tennyson—and in her own. The effort to achieve perfect diction took up much of Millay's creative energies.

Thus, partly modernist but mainly not, Millay remained considerably in the romantic poetic tradition. Yet she was responsive to the realistic drive of the times; she experimented in both meter and diction, and, as Minot took pains to demonstrate, her poetry did not remain static but developed in various ways. *The Buck in the Snow* and *Wine from These Grapes* show "definite major steps" in this development, which was gradual; but there are signs of it as early as 1921–23 with *Second April* and *The Harp-Weaver,* although her "new techniques supplemented rather than supplanted the old."[20]

This point comes out if one analyzes her work for inversions and archaisms. In her early poems there is some inversion of the sort that the modernists inveighed against. In all her poetry from first to last, she inverts normal sentence order, usually for emphasis, as most poets do. Occasionally she places adjectives after nouns, as in *whiteness uniform* (*CP,* 85), more frequently two adjectives after nouns, and, after a "Miltonic" fashion which appears rather more in later work than in early, adjectives both before and after nouns, as in *foreign daisies pink and small, the spongy radish coarse and hot, hanging leaves / Nerveless and darkened* (*CP,* 256, 330, 664). Predicate adjectives occasionally appear before verbs, and direct objects likewise, but most often, generally with emphatic effect, verbs before subjects, as in *swirled the dust, crashes the sleet from the bough, more sea than land am I, undefiled / Proceeds pure science* (*CP,* 8, 219, 279, 697).

In early poems Millay uses archaic forms like *fain, ere,* and *would that* fairly frequently, but with the years such forms appear less and less often—except in the first half of *Fatal Interview,* with its medieval atmosphere. She continued to use a few of these forms, however, such as *not* with a verb, as in *pity not, grieve not, be not haggard; do* as auxiliary with verbs, as in *I do fear, did change, nor did design; would* to express a wish, as in *I would be rid, would he had searched;* and *thee*'s and *thou*'s in a few very formal pieces.

On the other hand, Millay often wrote simply in the ballad style, and she was capable, early, of such colloquial poems as "The Bean-Stalk" *(Second April)*, "The Concert," and "Oh, oh, you will be sorry for that word" *(The Harp-Weaver)*. The short poems comprising "From a Very Little Sphinx" are also colloquial, carefully composed from a child's point of view. Millay adjusted her style according to theme and speaker of her poems; thus in the late "I woke in the night" *(CP,* 541) she herself speaks colloquially, *en dishabille* as it were. But of course, at other times and especially in sonnets, she is often more formal. Her versatility, variation, and development have not been sufficiently recognized.

Millay's death caused a number of appraisals to be published in 1950–51, the most sympathetic that of Rolfe Humphries, who attacked the prevailing attitude of depreciation. He thought her a fine lyric poet who could "write so memorably that her language was on every tongue" and who, in spite of occasional failures and shortcomings of taste and feeling, had wit and "clarity, mastery of epithet, control of modulation." In her later work "the lyric quality persisted, graver, more reflective, a little sorrowful for being wiser, a good deal subtler as the rhythms were moved to the more pensive mood."[21]

Criticism since her death has tended to find her work so tinged with the spirit of the 1920s that it is dated. Yet Millay told Elizabeth Breuer that readers liked her poetry because she wrote of things that most people had experienced, such as "love . . . / , / death, and nature, and the sea. Then, too, my images are homely, right out of the earth. . . . I have an age-old simplicity in the figures I employ."[22] Although Millay, like other poets, puts on different *personae,* the reader always perceives the woman who identifies herself by her compassion, her love of beauty, her idealism, her constant awareness of death, her fierce clinging to life, her unabashed treatment of love, her tough unwillingness to compromise, her vehement defense of what she considers right. Her sincere revelation of a modern woman is exact and strong, both in poems with physical setting and in more abstract works. As a woman writer she is in the tradition of Lizette Woodworth Reese, Anna Hempstead Branch, and Sara Teasdale, but she surpasses all of them in power and boldness. Millay's feminism served her well in breaking down conventionalities that they largely observed. Millay was responsible for destroying restrictions upon women's expression and prejudices against women's frankness. Although more women now participate in every sphere of life, women even yet are not so thoroughly emancipated, however, that Millay's feminism is dated. In addition, her feminine sensitivity both to beauty and to moral issues is one of the values of her work.

Without technical excellence these attitudes and ideas would mean nothing, of course, as poetry. In technique she bridges the time of Tennyson and the twentieth century. According to W. Adolphe Roberts, Tennyson and Housman were her acknowledged masters.[23] The Tennysonian and early Pre-Raphaelite attention to detail and sonority she adopted naturally. For use of the exact word and for subtle matchings of sound and sense her best work bears comparison with that of the finest masters of English poetic technique. Minot was impressed by her notable handling of the caesura. Although he felt that she suffered from a "general lack of architectonic skill," he praised "Renascence" and "Epitaph for the Race of Man" as her best longer pieces, and thought "her best sonnets and lyrics . . . as fine as any in the language."[24] She was at her mature best in elegiac poems, poems of precise description, and reflective sonnets. The philosophical sonnet sequence "Epitaph for the Race of Man," one of the great poems of the century,[25] is probably her highest achievement. Not far behind, although very different in subject, is "Sonnets from an Ungrafted Tree." *Fatal Interview,* a more ambitious undertaking, has more flaws, but Edmund Wilson, who was acute enough to write an excellent appreciation of *The Waste Land* when it first appeared, considered *Interview* "one of the great poems of our day."[26] Certain other works—the long, mystical "Renascence," the expressionistic poetic drama *Aria da Capo,* and the remarkable opera libretto *The King's Henchman*—are unique productions that stand out among the peaks of her success and illustrate the considerable range of her poetry.

Although Millay does not lack for readers, it is unfortunate that her mature work has not been adequately presented to the present generation in anthologies. In 1950 she complained that anthologists, picking poems they thought to have "the most popular appeal" (*Letters,* 371), reprinted only her "simple and youthful poems." She was criticizing the selections of F. O. Matthiessen for the *Oxford Book of American Verse.* But the whirligig of taste and the ascendancy of modernist editors have been responsible for more imbalance of poetic representation. Stanton

Coblentz caustically exposed the hewing to the party line of modernist critics and anthologists from 1955 to 1967.[27] Hardly any of the nonmodernist poets appeared in collections of that period. There has been no change yet. In the *New Oxford Book of American Verse* (1976), edited by Richard Ellmann, none of Millay's work is included—nor is any of Amy Lowell's or Elinor Wylie's. Albert Gelpi's 1973 anthology *The Poet in America,* heavily weighted on the post–World War II modernist side, also excludes Millay. But the anthologists' views are on all fours with the inaccuracies and eccentricities of various present-day critics.[28]

The high level of excellence that Millay reached in her sonnets did much to restore the sonnet to respectability during her time.[29] She especially deserves credit for success in the Petrarchan sonnet, which she wrote more and more with advancing years. She occasionally admits syntactical looseness and metaphorical inconsistency to her sonnets; but at her best, as Humphries indicated, she brought to the sonnet "much of the virtue of Latin elegy—the clarity, the point, the balance of sound, the limitation of sense—which she has studied with so much profit and so much affection."[30]

Although Millay is largely tied to tradition through sonnets, love lyrics, and ballads, her writing after 1928 is not bound to the traditional iambus and trochee or to traditional stanzas; she chooses her forms freely, sensitively exploring the possibilities of varied rhythms and lines of varied length. Winfield Townley Scott thought her work contained "a surprising number of ventures into free verse. . . ."[31] But, whatever her form, in the line of poets who stress predication,[32] she often uses long sentences with numerous qualifiers. Such sentences help to give a formal air to much of her poetry. Her eclectic genius created her great popularity and onetime fame; the critical neglect of her work that ensued is unjustified.[33] In fact, Millay is the greatest American lyrical poet of her century.

Millay's constant theme is devotion to freedom. The freedom of the individual, the freedom of woman completely to be an individual—these values engage her complete loyalty. Recent scholarship is scrutinizing Millay more intently as a *woman* poet subject to, suffering from, and both aware, and resentful, of the limitations, expectations, and humiliations that society has laid upon even its most gifted women.

Jane Stanbrough, for example (186ff.), points out how much the idea of
vulnerability (although often disguised by bravado) is expressed in
Millay's poems as well as her indignation over women's being subjected
to restriction, confinement, and assault. Feminist readers and critics are
finding that Millay has expressed, as few other poets have, "the
difficulty of being female in a male world, and the conflicting drives to
be at once a woman, some man's woman, and one's self."[34] To a study of
women's psychology Millay's work could make a large contribution.

She was not, of course, limited merely to the concerns of women, as
such works as *Aria da Capo* and "Epitaph for the Race of Man"
demonstrate. She had a permanent interest in the condition of humanity; yet she was "peculiarly a product of our native way of life."[35] We
might include her among our poets who "see New Englandly."[36] The
ideals of freedom and justice, paramount among the traditional values
of America, led her to denounce threats to these ideals. As a supporter
of freedom and justice she is a loyal citizen and a loyal critic of her
country although indignation occasionally betrays her into shrillness.
She became at times a prophetess-poet, never hesitating to speak her
mind on public matters—thoroughly American in the tradition of
Emerson, Whitman, Whittier, Lowell, and Moody. Yet, while pos-
sessing "a large sense of America," as Francis Hackett pointed out, she
also had a reverence for life that extended "beyond all sentient individual beings and so to universal being. . . ."[37] Every creature that
endures the pains and ecstasies of earthly life is awarded the dignity of
compassionate regard.

Hers is a radical creed. Meaningful freedom includes the freedom of
the human being to be himself, to retain his integrity and fearlessly to
express his individuality. Without belief in conventional religion Millay becomes a radical humanist, a Humanist-Stoic. Divisive modern
forces, atomistic in their effects, have impelled many twentieth-
century people along the same course. They find in Millay a poet who
provides a moving record of a full-bodied participant in the twentieth
century and who enunciates a credo for private lives and for public
issues.

Notes and References

Material from *Letters of Edna St. Vincent Millay* has not been noted.

Chapter One

1. Miriam Gurko, *Restless Spirit* (New York, 1962), pp. 24–26.
2. Toby Shafter, *Edna St. Vincent Millay* (New York, 1957), p. 59.
3. John Joseph Patton, *Edna St. Vincent Millay as a Verse Dramatist,* Ph.D. Diss., University of Colorado, 1962, pp. 35–37.
4. The sonnet was printed for the first time (along with commentary) in the Foreword to *Collected Sonnets of Edna St. Vincent Millay* (New York and London, 1941).
5. Gurko, *Restless,* p. 34.
6. William Wordsworth, Preface to *Lyrical Ballads.*
7. Gorham Munson, "'More Sea than Land Am I': Edna St. Vincent Millay and the Town of Camden," in *Penobscot: Down East Paradise* (Philadelphia: Lippincott, 1959), p. 234.
8. *Flowers of Evil* (New York and London, 1938), Preface, p. xxiii.
9. Letter of Ferdinand Earle to Arthur Davison Ficke, 3 December 1912, in the Arthur Davison Ficke Collection in the Yale University Library.
10. Ibid.
11. Jessie B. Rittenhouse, *My House of Life* (Boston: Houghton, Mifflin, 1934), p. 252.
12. Gurko, *Restless,* p. 50. That such an occasion provided the genesis of "Recuerdo" is also supported by Floyd Dell, Norma Millay, and W. Adolphe Roberts.
13. E. H. Haight, "Vincent at Vassar," *Vassar Alumnae Magazine* 36 (May 1951):14.
14. Henry Noble MacCracken, *The Hickory Limb* (New York: Scribner, 1950), pp. 211–12.
15. *The Fiftieth Anniversary of the Opening of Vassar College. October 10 to 13, 1915. A Record* (Poughkeepsie, N.Y., 1916), p. 234.
16. MacCracken, *The Hickory Limb,* p. 212.
17. Ibid., pp. 25–26, 92.

18. Max Eastman, *The Enjoyment of Living* (New York: Harper, 1948), p. 298.

19. Doris Stevens, *Jailed for Freedom* (New York: Boni and Liveright, 1920), p. 48.

20. The fullest account of the graduation difficulties is in Jean Gould, *The Poet and Her Book* (New York, 1969), pp. 63–68.

21. Helen Deutsch and Stella Hanau, *The Provincetown, A Story of the Theatre* (New York: Farrar and Rinehart, 1931), pp. 7, 20.

22. Floyd Dell, *Homecoming: An Autobiography* (New York: Farrar and Rinehart, 1933), p. 299.

23. Sheldon Cheney, *The Art Theatre*, rev. ed. (New York: Knopf, 1925), p. 68.

24. Gould, *Poet*, pp. 83, 87.

25. Information given me by Norma Millay, 4 July 1964.

26. Malcolm Cowley, *Exile's Return* (New York: Norton, 1934), pp. 57–58.

27. Frederick J. Hoffman, *The Twenties* (New York: Viking, 1955), p. 35.

28. Cowley, *Exile's*, p. 59.

29. Information in private letters to me from Floyd Dell and Edmund Wilson.

30. Cowley, *Exile's*, pp. 69–71.

31. Dell, *Homecoming*, p. 301.

32. Llewelyn Powys, "Mr. Dell Gazes Wistfully Out upon Life," *New York Times Book Review* 20 (20 April 1924):14.

33. A. D. Ficke, *Selected Poems* (New York: Doran, 1926), p. 182.

34. According to a Ficke letter at Steepletop, he sailed 19 February 1918.

35. It is number 14 among Ficke's copies of Millay's sonnets in the Arthur Davison Ficke Collection in the Yale University Library. It was published in *Reedy's Mirror* and in Houston Peterson's *The Book of Sonnet Sequences* (New York: Longmans, 1929), but not collected later.

36. In line 4 the poet replaced *fire* with *flame* and *white* with *sharp*.

37. W. Adolphe Roberts, "Tiger Lily" (unpublished memoir of Millay in the Vassar College Library), p. 3.

38. Ibid., pp. 2–7, 9–10, 17–18.

39. For Middleton, Millay wrote the classically inspired "To S. M. (If He Should Lie A-Dying)."

40. Floyd Dell, "My Friend Edna St. Vincent Millay," *Mark Twain Journal* 12 (Spring 1964):2.

41. Gurko, *Restless*, pp. 93–97.

42. Grace King, *The Development . . . of Edna St. Vincent Millay* (Ph.D. Diss., New York University, 1943), p. 166.

43. Lawrence Langner, *The Magic Curtain* (New York: Dutton, 1951), p. 120.

44. King, *Development,* p. 100.

45. Edmund Wilson, *The Shores of Light* (New York, 1952), p. 751. Probably John Peale Bishop wrote poems with Millay in mind; cf. "Song" and "I Lean upon the Night," in *The Collected Poems of John Peale Bishop,* ed. with a Preface and a Personal Memoir by Allen Tate (New York, 1948), pp. 263–64, 276–77.

46. Edmund Wilson, *I Thought of Daisy* (New York: Scribner, 1929), p. 17.

47. Wilson, *Shores of Light,* p. 766.

48. Frank Crowninshield, "Crowninshield in the Cubs' Den," *Vogue* 104 (1 November 1944):158.

49. The other three were Henry Carter, Stanley Hawks, and Stephen Vincent Benét, to whom Vincent was known as Jerry. Cf. *Selected Letters of Stephen Vincent Benét,* ed. Charles A. Fenton (New Haven: Yale University Press, 1960), p. 26.

50. Dell, in a private letter, 26 December 1963, wrote that Millay told Doris Stevens of the affair, that Esther Root, whom Millay knew in Paris, said that Millay had not told the father of her pregnancy, and that Millay told Gladys Brown Ficke that the story was correct. Dell gave similar information to Miriam Gurko and Emily Hahn, who included it in "Mostly about Vincent," in *Romantic Rebels: An Informal History of Bohemianism in America* (Boston: Houghton, Mifflin, 1967), p. 239.

51. Grace Hegger Lewis, *With Love from Gracie* (New York: Harcourt, Brace, 1955), p. 197.

52. Dell's letter of 26 December 1963.

53. Information given me by Charles Ellis, 4 July 1964.

54. These were numbered as follows in *The Harp-Weaver and Other Poems:* 1, 12, 4, 9, 19, 22, 8, 11.

55. John Hohenberg, *The Pulitzer Prizes* (New York: Columbia University Press, 1974), pp. 69–70.

56. Joseph Freeman, *An American Testament* (New York: Farrar and Rinehart, 1936), pp. 246–47.

57. Gould, *Poet,* 156–57; and cf. Dell, *Homecoming,* p. 398.

58. Eastman, *Enjoyment,* p. 521; *New York Times,* 31 August 1949; *New York Herald Tribune,* 31 August 1949; Dell, *Homecoming,* p. 309; Wilson, *The Shores of Light,* p. 771; Allan Ross Macdougall, "Husband of a Genius," *Delineator* 125 (October 1934):41.

59. Dell, *Homecoming,* p. 398.

60. A tentative contract drawn up by Ficke is in the Arthur Davison Ficke Collection in the Yale University Library.

61. Ficke wrote this in January 1924. Manuscript in the Arthur Davison Ficke Collection.

62. In the Arthur Davison Ficke Collection there is a telegram of this date from Millay to Ficke.

63. *Commemorative Tributes of the American Academy of Arts and Letters, 1942–1951:* "Edna St. Vincent Millay" by Deems Taylor, p. 107.

64. *New Yorker* 3 (19 February 1927):18.

65. Adams awarded her a watch for the best contribution of the year. The poem was reprinted in the *Literary Digest,* 19 December 1925.

66. John J. Patton, *Edna St. Vincent Millay as a Verse Dramatist,* pp. 156–57; Gurko, *Restless,* pp. 175–77. 175–77.

67. *Survey* 57 (15 November 1926):205; Gurko, *Restless,* p. 181.

68. *New York Times,* 5 May 1927, p. 12; 6 May 1927, p. 25; 7 May 1927, p. 4.

69. Ibid., 28 July 1926, p. 1; 4 August 1927, p. 1.

70. Ibid., 5 August 1927, pp. 1, 4, 5; 6 August 1927, p. 2; 7 August 1927, pp. 1, 23; 8 August 1927, p. 2.

71. Ibid., 9 August 1927, pp. 1, 3–4; 10 August 1927, pp. 1–2; 11 August 1927, pp. 1, 3; Jeannette Marks, *Thirteen Days* (New York: A. & C. Boni, 1929), pp. 1–2, 8, 9–10; Michael A. Musmanno, *After Twelve Years* (New York: Knopf, 1939), p.303.

72. *New York Times,* 21 August 1927, Sec. 1, p. 18.

73. First published in the *Liberator,* October 1922; reprinted in *May Days; an anthology of Verse from Masses-Liberator,* ed. Genevieve Taggard (New York, 1925), p. 187.

74. *New York Times,* 22 August 1927, pp. 1–2; Musmanno, *After,* pp. 341–43; Marks, *Thirteen,* p. 26.

75. Katherine Anne Porter, *The Never-Ending Wrong* (Boston: Little, Brown, 1977), pp. 50–51. The photograph faces p. 32.

76. *New York Times,* 23 August 1927, p. 4; Marks, *Thirteen,* pp. 28–30; Musmanno, *After,* pp. 387–88; Arthur Garfield Hays, *Let Freedom Ring,* rev. ed. (New York: Boni and Liveright, 1937), pp. 337–38.

77. *New York Times,* 24 August 1927, p. 2; *Letters of Edna St. Vincent Millay* (New York and London, 1952), pp. 223–24.

78. *New York Times,* 25 August 1927, p. 10; Karl Yost, *A Bibliography of the Works of Edna St. Vincent Millay* (New York, 1937), pp. 62–65.

79. William Miller, *A New History of the United States* (New York: Braziller, 1958), pp. 350–56.

80. King, *Development,* pp. 5, 6, 132, 138–39.

81. Jerome Beatty, "Best Sellers in Verse: the Story of Edna St. Vincent

Millay," *American Magazine* 113 (January 1932):103.

82. Allan Ross Macdougall, "Husband of a Genius," *Delineator* 125 (October 1934):40–41.

83. Gould, *Poet,* p. 162; Joan Dash, *A Life of One's Own: Three Gifted Women and the Men They Married* (New York, 1973), p. 171.

84. Dash, *Life,* p. 183.

85. Beatty, "Best Sellers," pp. 102–4.

86. Wilson, *Shores of Light,* pp. 790–91.

87. Cablegram in the Yale University Library.

88. Information from George Dillon in a private letter of 24 April 1964.

89. There is a hint, although at once disclaimed, about Dillon as the lover in Gould, *Poet,* p. 202. Very few outside of a small circle of the Boissevains' intimates knew of the affair until Fanny Butcher, reporter and columnist who wrote about books and authors for Chicago newspapers, asserted that after Dillon's death a copy of *Fatal Interview* in his library was found to have an inscription by Millay: "These are all for you, my darling." *Many Lives—One Love* (New York: Harper and Row, 1972), p. 75. But her report was not quite accurate. Alice Baur Hodges, Dillon's cousin and literary executor, says that Millay's note was on a sheet of paper inserted in the book. Mrs. Hodges told Dillon's close friend Arthur Meeker in confidence of this discovery, and she believes that Meeker let Fanny Butcher know about it. Information from Alice Baur Hodges by telephone, 25 March 1980 and 8 January 1981.

90. *New York Times,* 17 December 1928, pp. 23, 27; Gould, *Poet,* p. 198.

91. Mr. Millay was buried at Bangor on 24 December 1935. For reasons of health, Vincent, who was in Delray Beach, Fla., and Norma did not go to Bangor. Eugen went, made arrangements, and attended the funeral. Cf. issues of 24 December 1935, *Bangor Daily News, Bangor Daily Commercial, New York Times,* p. 15. I am indebted to Walter S. Minot for these references.

92. Letter of 25 June 1963 from Floyd Dell.

93. Max Eastman, "My Friendship with Edna Millay," *Great Companions* (New York, 1959), p. 103.

94. King, *Development,* p. 143.

95. Ibid., p. 203.

96. Wilson, *Shores of Light,* p. 787; Eastman, *Great Companions,* pp. 101–2; Harrison Dowd in an interview of 14 June 1964.

97. Anne Cheney, *Millay in Greenwich Village* (University, Ala., 1975), p. 126.

98. Dash, *A Life of One's Own,* pp. 221, 227.

99. Letter in the New York Public Library.

Chapter Two

1. Louis Untermeyer, *The New Era in American Poetry* (New York: Holt, 1919), p. 272.
2. Harriet Monroe, "First Books of Verse," *Poetry* 13 (December 1918):167.
3. Walter S. Minot, *Edna St. Vincent Millay: A Critical Revaluation* (Ph.D. diss., University of Nebraska, 1972), p. 127.
4. Donald Smalley, "Millay's 'Renascence' and Browning's 'Easter Day,'" *Bulletin of the Maine Library Association* 3 (February 1942):10–12.
5. Louis Untermeyer, *American Poetry Since 1900* (New York, 1923), p. 214; Dell, *Literary Spotlight*, p. 86; Davison, "Edna St. Vincent Millay," pp. 675–76.
6. Untermeyer, *New Era in American Poetry*, p. 274.
7. Jean Morris Petitt, *Edna St. Vincent Millay: A Critical Study of Her Poetry in its Social and Literary Milieu* (Ph.D. diss., Vanderbilt University, 1955), p. 123. Edmund Wilson thinks that the storm in "Renascence" also stands for sexual love. *Shores of Light*, p. 759.
8. Seventy-two out of 171 published sonnets are Petrarchan; and there are others with the Petrarchan sestet.
9. King, *Development*, p. 82.
10. Cf. Seneca, *Hippolytus*, 1. 607: *Curae leves loquuntur, ingentes stupent* ("Light troubles speak; great ones are dumb").
11. Van Doren, *Many Minds*, p. 110.
12. *Literary Spotlight*, p. 81.
13. Cowley, *Exile's*, pp. 223–24.
14. Llewellyn Jones, *First Impressions* (New York: Knopf, 1925), p. 113.
15. Carl Van Doren compared her poems to Suckling's. *Many Minds* (New York, 1924), p. 111.
16. Hutchins Hapgood, *The Story of a Lover* (New York: Boni and Liveright, 1919), pp. 105–7.
17. In Yost, *Bibliography*, p. 19.
18. O. W. Firkins, "'Second April' (An October View)," *Independent* 107 (19 November 1921):194.
19. Colum, "Miss Millay's Poems," p. 189.
20. Wilson, *Shores of Light*, p. 759.
21. In Yost, *Bibliography*, p. 23.
22. Bynner, *New Republic*, p. 14.
23. Maxwell Anderson, *Measure*, no. 7 (September 1921), p. 17.

24. Colum, "Miss Millay's Poems," p. 189.

25. Alfred Kreymborg, *Our Singing Strength* (New York, 1929), p. 442.

26. Walter Gierasch relates the imagery of the poem to Ecclesiastes. *Explicator* 2 (May 1944):23.

27. Gurko, *Restless,* p. 63. At Vassar, Millay publicly recited the Latin poem.

28. Not understanding the Roman context, Minot, p. 166, was wrong to say that stanza 3 is "too light and flippant."

29. This line (*Inferno,* 5:113) comes from Dante's pitying comment after he has heard the first part of Francesca's explanation of her love affair with Paolo: "What sweet thoughts, what desire led these lovers into this painful pass." After his comment Francesca tells how she and Paolo were reading the book of Lancelot mentioned at the end of Millay's sonnet.

30. Colum, "Miss Millay's Poems," p. 189.

31. See note 18 above.

32. Minot, *Edna St. Vincent Millay,* pp. 147–48.

33. Davison, "Edna St. Vincent Millay," p. 678.

34. Elizabeth P. Perlmutter, "A Doll's Heart: The Girl in the Poetry of Edna St. Vincent Millay and Louise Bogan," *Twentieth Century Literature* 23 (1977):157–79.

35. Minot, *Edna St. Vincent Millay,* p. 108.

36. The publication date shows that Sonnet 16 cannot have been written, as Dell supposed, after Millay heard of John Reed's death in 1920.

37. George Sarton, *A History of Science, II: Hellenistic Science and Culture in the Last Three Centuries B. C.* (Cambridge, Mass.: Harvard, 1959) p. 39.

38. Wilson, *Shores of Light,* p. 780.

39. The Arthur Davison Ficke Collection in the Yale University Library. See also Floyd Dell's review of Ficke's *Out of Silence, and Other Poems* in *Measure,* 42 (August 1924), p. 12.

Chapter Three

1. Note the reference to Jim in *Letters of Edna St. Vincent Millay,* p. 131.

2. The heroine is called Melisande McIlravy. One of Millay's Vassar classmates was Alice Pauline McIlravy, of Tarrytown, N.Y. Floyd Dell informed me that he called Millay by the pet names of Melusine and Melisande.

3. *The King's Henchman,* p. 15, has a reference to the "rich hue" of an embroidered peacock's eye.

4. Gurko, *Restless Spirit,* pp. 92–96.

5. Vincent Sheean, *The Indigo Bunting: A Memoir of Edna St. Vincent Millay* (New York, 1951), p. 51.

6. In a leter from Paris (18 March 1921), Millay reminded Norma, her collaborator on this story, of how hard they worked to finish the novelette.

7. Another story, "Pepper, Mostly," was bought by *Ainslee's* in 1919 but never published. (Information in a letter of 23 August 1963 from Condé Nast Publications, Inc., which acquired the copyrights of material published in *Ainslee's.*)

8. *Letters,* pp. 118–20, 121.

9. The foregoing material is taken, with slight alterations, from my article "Edna St. Vincent Millay's 'Nancy Boyd' Stories," *Ball State University Forum* 10 (Spring 1969):31–36; copyright 1969 by *Ball State University Forum;* reprinted by permission.

10. Northrop Frye, *Anatomy of Criticism* (Princeton, N.J.: Princeton University Press, 1957), p. 309.

11. Alvin Kernan, *The Cankered Muse* (New Haven: Yale University Press, 1959), p. 13.

12. John J. Patton, "Satiric Fiction in Millay's *Distressing Dialogues,*" *Modern Language Studies* 2 (Summer 1972):63, 65.

13. Published in *Century* 105 (March 1923):663–75.

14. Cf. *Letters,* p. 165.

15. But concerning her "Nancy Boyd" pieces Millay told Elizabeth Breuer: "I know they sound as if they tripped off my typewriter, but I had such anguish of mind over them, so much preparation went into them that even now I could say some of them off by heart. . . .

"I am a very careful and deliberate writer." "Edna St. Vincent Millay," *Pictorial Review* 33 (November 1931):52.

Chapter Four

1. Preface to *The Princess Marries the Page* (New York and London, 1932), p. xi.

2. Ibid., p. xii.

3. The play has a few touches reminiscent of the style of Beulah Marie Dix. See Patton, *Edna St. Vincent Millay,* pp. 70–71.

4. Ibid., p. 47.

5. Haight, "Vincent at Vassar."

6. Cf. Millay's production notes in the Walter Baker edition, pp. 39–48. A typescript of these notes is in the Vassar College Library.

7. King, *Development,* p. 100.

8. Information from Floyd Dell in a letter of 25 June 1963.

9. Robert Emmons Rogers, *Behind a Watteau Picture* (Boston: Walter H. Baker, 1918), p. 62.

10. She had a part in *Jack's House.* Kreymborg, *Troubadour,* pp. 314–16.

11. Alexander Woollcott, *New York Times,* 14 December 1919, Sec. 8, p. 2.

12. Harriet Monroe, *Poetry* 24 (August 1924):264; 30 (April 1927):46; Van Doren, *Many Minds,* p. 110; Kreymborg, *Our Singing Strength,* p. 445; Rica Brenner, *Ten Modern Poets* (New York, 1930), p. 74; Dell, *Homecoming,* p. 267; Atkins, *Edna St. Vincent Millay,* p. 77; Oscar Cargill, *Intellectual America: Ideas on the March* (New York, 1941), p. 641.

13. In Yost, *Bibliography,* p. 48; Patton, *Edna St. Vincent Millay,* p. 124; Edmund Wilson had felt "thrilled and troubled" by the play, which provided not only "a bitter treatment of war" but also "a less common sense of the incongruity and cruelty of life, of the precariousness of love perched on a table above the corpses . . . , and renewing its eternal twitter in the silence that succeeded the battle." *Shores of Light,* pp. 748–49.

14. Frank Shay, Foreword to *Contemporary Plays of 1921* (American) (Cincinnati, 1922), p. 6.

15. Alan S. Downer, *Fifty Years of American Drama: 1900–1950* (Chicago: Regnery, 1951), p. 47.

16. Atkins, *Edna St. Vincent Millay,* pp. 38–40; Patton, *Edna St. Vincent Millay,* p. 142.

17. Cf. Cook, in Yost, *Bibliography,* pp. 47–48; Agnes Kendrick Gray, *Measure,* no. 7 (September 1921), p. 18.

18. *New Yorker* 3 (26 February 1927):61; (5 March 1927):68, 69.

19. Lee Simonson, "Minority Report," in *Minor Prophecies* (New York: Harcourt, Brace, 1927), pp. 119–20, 126–29, 134.

20. Edward Johnson, "English Is Beautiful and Singable," *Musical Observer* 26 (October 1927):11.

21. Mary F. Watkins, "Operatic Events of the Last Month," *Musical Observer* 26 (April 1927):38–39; Arthur Hobson Quinn, *A History of the American Drama from the Civil War to the Present Day,* rev. ed. (New York: Crofts, 1937), 2:148–50; Patton, *Edna St. Vincent Millay,* pp. 159–68.

Chapter Five

1. Louis Untermeyer, "Songs from Thistles," *Saturday Review of Literature* 5 (13 Oct. 1928):209.

2. The copy in the Arthur Davison Ficke Collection has a few differences of punctuation from the published version: line 12 has a semicolon after

steady; line 17 a semicolon after *roses*. Line 18 ends with four ellipsis periods, and there is no space between lines 18 and 19. Line 19 has no comma after the second *alone*.

3. Minot, *Edna St. Vincent Millay,* pp. 140–41.

4. In Yost, *Bibliography,* p. 38.

5. Late in 1930 Llewelyn Powys wrote from Steepletop to his sister: "We here have lately been tormented by shooting people. It has been the open season lasting a fortnight and we have seen no less than 11 stags carried away on the backs of motor cars. It is a shame, if only they would go into the next state they would be safe." *Letters of Llewelyn Powys* (London: John Lane, 1943), p. 158.

6. Wilson, *Shores of Light,* p. 773.

7. Untermeyer praised the sonnet—in spite of "its almost fatal first line"—as "that rarest of things, a successful poem on a symphony." *Modern American Poetry,* p. 484; Mid-Century ed., p. 458.

8. Patricia A. Klemans, "'Being Born a Woman': A New Look at Edna St. Vincent Millay," *Colby Library Quarterly* 15 (March 1979):16.

9. Ibid., p. 13.

10. In lines 9–11 Millay translates the medieval student song *Gaudeamus Igitur:*

> *Gaudeamus igitur, juvenes dum sumus.*
> *Post jucundam juventutem,*
> *Post molestam senectutem*
> *Nos habebit humus.*

11. Klemans, "'Being Born a Woman,'" p. 8.

12. Minot, *Edna St. Vincent Millay,* p. 43. The love debate of Sonnets 18, 19, 22, and 30, as in Sidney's sonnets, is another Renaissance element.

13. Cook, in Yost, *Bibliography,* p. 43.

14. For an analysis of Sonnet 11 see Francis X. Curley, "Edna St. Vincent Millay," *America* 84 (11 November 1950):166–68.

15. Millay told Wilson in 1948 that she had lost the first draft of that poem. *Shores of Light,* pp. 769, 787.

16. With the notation "This sonnet to be italicized," the typescript of "Epitaph" in the Arthur Davison Ficke Collection opens with:

> Have you a townsman somewhere in the crowd,
> To urge the wise, deplore the foolish deed,
> Giving you counsel that you wll not heed,
> O Hero? . . . and to groan your wounds aloud?
> A simple citizen and unendowed

> With prophecy, but who would have you freed
> Straightway from error, knowing what's decreed,
> And seeing you too thoughtless and so proud?
> Let him remain in shadow and rehearse
> Your former state, the glories of your line;
> Tell how the gods grew angry, of the curse
> They forged, of how you bled and gave no sign;
> And how these matters went from bad to worse,
> Your sword being mortal and the curse divine.

In the typescript sonnets 3 and 8 do not appear. "What rider spurs him from the darkening east," printed as the final sonnet in *Collected Poems,* was number 7 (thus bringing together poems on Egypt and Nineveh), and was followed by sonnets 12 and 13. The introduction of Sonnet 3 was necessary to move from the time of dinosaurs to the origin of mammalian life; Sonnet 8 added earthquake to the disasters surmounted by Man; and sonnets 12–13 have a better position, after more human development, much later than the primitive time of the "coughing tiger." The most notable textual change is in lines 5–6 of Sonnet 2, which were originally much less distinctive:

> Spring passed, and summer came; the sky was blue;
> Rain fell and there was fog; the sky was grey.

17. King, *Development,* p. 144.

18. Minot, *Edna St. Vincent Millay,* p. 84.

19. On 5 December 1934, Millay told reporters that she was "disillusioned and embittered." *New York Post,* 5 December 1934, p. 5.

20. In the typescript of this poem in the Arthur Davison Ficke Collection, *Libra* of line 8 replaced *Rigel,* which replaced the original *Vega.*

21. Benét, "Round About," p. 279; Louise Bogan, "Conversion into Self," *Poetry* 45 (February 1935):277–78; P. B. Rice, "Edna Millay's Maturity," *Nation* 139 (14 November 1934):568; Cook, in Yost, *Bibliography,* p. 45; Hildegarde Flanner, "Two Poets: Jeffers and Millay," in *After the Genteel Tradiiton: American Writers since 1910,* ed. Malcolm Cowley (New York: Norton, 1937), p. 165.

22. *Flowers of Evil,* pp. vii, x, xi–xii.

23. Millay, *Flowers of Evil,* pp. xx, xxiv, xxv, xxxiv. Note also Dillon's "Reply with Rejoinder to Mary Colum's Article 'Edna Millay and Her Time,'" *New Republic* 124 (23 April 1951):4.

24. Cf. Arnold Whitridge, "Baudelaire in English," *Yale Review,* n.s., 25 (Summer 1936):823; Tate, "Eleven Words for Seven," *Nation* 143 (4 July 1936):22.

25. John P. Bishop, "A Diversity of Opinions," *Poetry* 51 (November 1937):104.

26. Wilson, "Give That Beat Again," *Shores of Light,* p. 684.

27. In a letter to Ficke, 2 November 1938 (in the Arthur Davison Ficke Collection in the Yale University Library), Joseph Freeman suggested a resemblance between *Conversation* and Ficke's *Mr. Faust.* This resemblance is limited to a similarity of scene—a wealthy man's house where a discussion occurs. Millay dedicated the book "To Arthur Davison Ficke and 42 Commerce Street," the address of Ficke's studio in the early 1920s. Llewelyn Powys knew in November 1936 of the dedication. *Letters of Llewelyn Powys,* p. 212.

28. Secretary of Commerce Herbert Hoover had called a conference of munitions makers to advise the American delegation to the League of Nations. Things they objected to were kept out of the treaty. *New York Evening Journal,* 5 December 1934, p. 17.

29. Michel Mok, "Poetic Strife Begins at 42 for Edna St. Vincent Millay," *New York Post,* 5 December 1934, p. 5. The phrase "a thousand well-wishers breathe on my neck" shows that she was thinking of, if not writing, *Conversation at Midnight.* The expression appears, slightly altered, in the volume. In fact, the sonnet "Being out of love and out of mood with loving" had appeared in the *Saturday Evening Post* as early as 6 December 1930. Possibly *Conversation* had gradually been taking shape in her mind for several years.

30. Clipping from an unidentified newspaper in the W. Adolphe Roberts scrapbook in the Vassar College Library.

31. Patton, *Edna St. Vincent Millay,* pp. 204–6; Bishop, *Poetry* 51 (November 1937):101; Thomas Caldecott Chubb, "Shelley Grown Old," *North American Review* 245 (September 1938):178.

32. One should recall the Russian trials and "purges" of August 1936 and January 1937.

33. King, *Development,* p. 150; Patton, *Edna St. Vincent Millay,* pp. 209–10.

34. Patton, *Edna St. Vincent Millay,* pp. 176–92.

35. Archibald MacLeish, *Panic* (Boston and New York: Houghton, Mifflin, 1935), pp. 48–49.

36. Patton, *Edna St. Vincent Millay,* pp. 195–96.

37. Ibid., p. 198.

38. A copy of the ballad dated 17 April 1934 was sent to Powys with the title "For L. P." from the Cove Hotel, Lulworth Cove, Dorset. It is in the Yale University Library. *Huntsman, What Quarry?* was dedicated to Powys and his wife, Alyse Gregory.

39. Paul Rosenfeld, "Under Angry Constellations," *Poetry* 55 (October 1939):48.

40. King, *Development,* pp. 234–35.

41. She mentioned it in a letter to Dillon, 23 March 1939.

42. Millay discussed the poem with George Dillon; "secret body" instead of "quiet body" was his suggestion. *Letters of Edna St. Vincent Millay,* p. 301.

43. *New York Herald Tribune,* 25 October 1939, p. 11. The United States Neutrality Act was amended 3 November 1939 so as to repeal the embargo on arms.

44. Millay explained her position in a long letter (2 January 1941) to her protesting friend, Mrs. Charlotte Babcock Sills.

45. Note of 4 September 1941 on preface to *Collected Sonnets,* in the Arthur Davison Ficke Collection in the Yale University Library.

46. King, *Development,* p. 227.

47. In addition, the volume contains "Journal," a sort of miscellany written in the 1920s, and three poems on legendary figures: Tristan, Alcestis (in a feminist position), and Penelope.

48. In Yost, *Bibliography,* p. 54.

49. Louise Townsend Nicholl, "A Late, Rich Harvest of Edna Millay," *New York Herald Tribune Books,* 23 May 1954, p. 5.

50. One suspects that Millay found her imagination stirred on this subject after she made a hurried, brief reply in 1937 or early 1938 to questions from *Books Abroad* about her reading: "Before I was ten years old, I had read almost every word of Shakespeare. . . . I had also read *Don Quixote,* Christopher Marlowe's *Hero and Leander,* a great deal of Alexander Pope, Grimm's *Fairy Tales, Alice in Wonderland,* the poems of Tennyson, Jean Ingelow, and Milton." *Books Abroad* 12 (Spring 1938):165.

51. Breuer, "Edna St. Vincent Millay," p. 54.

52. King, *Development,* pp. 234, 235.

Chapter Six

1. Ellen Key, *The Woman Movement* (New York: Putnam, 1912; preface dated 1909), pp. 112–26.

2. Havelock Ellis, *Man and Woman,* 5th ed. (New York: Scribner, 1915 [1st ed., 1894]), pp. 17–18, 520–21.

3. Scott and Nellie M. S. Nearing, *Woman and Social Progress* (New York: Macmillan, 1912), p. xii.

4. June Sochen, *The New Woman: Feminism in Greenwich Village, 1910–1920* (New York: Quadrangle Books, 1972), p. ix.

5. Ibid., p. 47.

6. Henry Noble MacCracken, *The Hickory Limb* (New York: Scribner, 1950), p. 91.

7. Agnes Rogers, *Vassar Women. An Informal Study* (Poughkeepsie, N.Y.: Vassar College, 1940), p. 67.

8. Margaret Widdemer, *Golden Friends I Had* (Garden City, N.Y.: Doubleday, 1964), p. 24.

9. Louis Untermeyer, *Modern American and British Poetry* (New York: Harcourt, Brace, 1943), 2:298.

10. Edna G. Rostow, "Conflict and Accommodation," in *The Woman in America,* ed. Robert Jay Lifton (Boston: Houghton, Mifflin, 1965), p. 213.

11. Floyd Dell, *Love in Greenwich Village* (New York, 1926: reprinted, Freeport, N.Y.: Books for Libraries Press, 1970), p. 72.

12. Sochen, *New Woman,* p. 31.

13. Dell, *Homecoming,* p. 304.

14. Carl N. Degler, "The Changing Place of Women in America," in *The Woman in America,* pp. 197–98.

15. Sochen, *New Woman,* p. 40.

16. Millay, "The Pioneer," *Equal Rights,* 24 November 1923, p. 327.

17. Florence Kelley, "The New Woman's Party," *Survey* 45 (5 March 1921):827–28.

18. Gould, *The Poet,* pp. 177–78.

19. Gurko, *Restless,* p. 169.

Chapter Seven

1. Millay was accused of self-conscious flippancy, ignoble adroitness, unworthy cuteness, pseudosophisticated smartness. See Untermeyer, *American Poetry Since 1900,* p. 217; Kreymborg, *Our Singing Strength,* p. 441; Clement Wood, *Poets of America* (New York: Dutton, 1925), pp. 203–12; McInnis, "The New Writers," p. 424. Sister Madeleva, however, said that Millay had "let a gust of gay and impudent laughter in upon the feverish sentimentalism of the day" (p. 150).

2. Davison, "Edna St. Vincent Millay," pp. 672–81.

3. Blankenship, "Edna St. Vincent Millay," p. 626; Parks, *American Literature,* pp. 46–48.

4. McInnis, "The New Writers," pp. 424–25.

5. Ludwig Lewisohn, *The Story of American Literature* (New York: Harper, 1932), p. 580.

6. "Miss Millay's Sonnets," *New Republic* 66 (6 May 1931):335–36.

7. Wilson, "The Literary Worker's Polonius," in *Shores of Light,* p. 605; originally in *Atlantic Monthly,* June 1935.

8. Minot, *Edna St. Vincent Millay,* p. 2.

9. T. E. Hulme, "Lecture on Modern Poetry," in *Further Speculations by T. E. Hulme,* ed. Sam Hynes (Minneapolis: University of Minnesota Press, 1955), pp. 73, 75.

10. David Perkins, *A History of Modern Poetry from the 1890s to the High Modernist Mode* (Cambridge, Mass. and London: Harvard, 1976), p. 306.

11. W. H. Auden, *The Dyer's Hand and Other Essays* (New York: Random House, 1962), p. 84.

12. Perkins, *History,* pp. 298, 310, 299.

13. Ibid., p. 308.

14. Yvor Winters, *Primitivism and Decadence: A Study of American Experimental Poetry,* in *In Defense of Reason* (New York: Morrow, 1947), p. 87.

15. Klemans, "'Being Born a Woman,'" p. 11.

16. Herbert Read, *Letter to a Young Painter* (London: Thames, 1962), p. 64.

17. Monroe K. Spears, *Dionysus and the City* (New York: Oxford University Press, 1970), p. 25.

18. John H. Wheelock, *American Poetry at Mid-Century,* quoted in Jay B. Hubbell, *Who Are the Major American Writers?* (Durham, N.C.: Duke University Press, 1972), p. 234. It is ironic that with the 1960s the whirligig brought the "confessional" poets into favor.

19. *Further Speculations by T. E. Hulme,* p. 71.

20. Minot, *Edna St. Vincent Millay,* pp. 161–62. In 1956 or 57 Joseph Warren Beach placed Millay among poets of her generation who were "all more or less innovators in form and style." *Obsessive Images,* ed. William Van O'Connor (Minneapolis: University of Minnesota Press, 1960), p. 370.

21. Rolfe Humphries, "Edna St. Vincent Millay, 1892–1950," *Nation* 171 (20 December 1950):704.

22. Breuer, "Edna St. Vincent Millay," p. 50.

23. W. A. Roberts, "Tiger Lily," unpublished memoir in the Vassar College Library, pp. 11, 14.

24. Minot, *Edna St. Vincent Millay,* pp. 209, 211, 212, 216.

25. "I know of nothing in American literature to compare in scope and grandeur of intellectual grasp and eloquence with her 'Epitaph for the Race of Man.' . . . the only poem in the language since Milton that can be compared in mental boldness, with Dante and Lucretius. . . ." Eastman, *Great Companions,* p. 83.

26. Wilson, *Shores of Light,* p. 779.

27. Stanton Coblentz, "Freedom through Dictatorship," in *The Poetry Circus* (New York: Hawthorn Books, 1967), pp. 172–84. "There is a clamping down of a viselike conformity. There is a denial of the freedom to

depart from the prescriptions of the reigning clique." p. 184.

28. For example, the sweeping statement of Hyatt Waggoner, "all her statements came to have a quality of shrillness," in *American Poets from the Puritans to the Present* (Boston: Houghton, Mifflin, 1968), p. 467; Bette Richart's claim that Millay "did not experiment at all with form," "Poet of Our Youth," *Commonweal* 66 (10 May 1957):151; the accusation of John McCormick that "bloodlessness" (!) is characteristic of much of Millay's poetry, *The Middle Distance: A Comparative History of American Imaginative Literature* (New York: Free Press, 1971), p. 160; Wilbur M. Frohock's notion that apart from "the devil-may-care, bohemian hedonist *persona* . . . there is astonishingly little sign of anything like revolt in her work," "Edna St. Vincent Millay: Little Girl Lost," in *Strangers to This Ground* (Dallas: Southern Methodist University Press, 1961), p. 95.

29. Floyd Dell, "The Ficke Wing," *Measure* 42 (August 1924):12–13.

30. Humphries, "Miss Millay as Artist," *Nation* 153 (20 December 1941):644.

31. Scott, "Millay Collected," p. 340.

32. Josephine Miles, *Eras and Modes in English Poetry* (Berkeley: University of California Press, 1964), pp. 27, 261.

33. Minot, *Edna St. Vincent Millay,* p. 206.

34. Dash, *A Life of One's Own,* p. xviii.

35. Gray, *Edna St. Vincent Millay,* p. 44.

36. To "see New Englandly" is "to be versed in country things, the land and the life on the land . . ." and to "see morally, didactically . . . , the eye reading nature and society as manuals of instruction, facts flowering into truths of conduct." William Mulder, "Seeing 'New Englandly': Planes of Perception in Emily Dickinson and Robert Frost," *New England Quarterly* 52 (1979):550.

37. Hackett, "Edna St. Vincent Millay," p. 21.

Selected Bibliography

PRIMARY SOURCES

Prefaces and musical settings by Millay are not cited.

1. Collections of Poetry

Renascence and Other Poems. New York: Mitchell Kennerley, 1917.

A Few Figs from Thistles. Poems and Four Sonnets. Salvo One. New York: Frank Shay, 1920. Enlarged editions, 1921, 1922.

Second April. New York: Mitchell Kennerley, 1921.

The Harp-Weaver and Other Poems. New York and London: Harper and Brothers, 1923.

The Buck in the Snow. New York and London: Harper and Brothers, 1928.

Edna St. Vincent Millay's Poems Selected for Young People. New York and London: Harper and Brothers, 1929.

Fatal Interview. Sonnets by Edna St. Vincent Millay. New York and London: Harper and Brothers, 1931.

Wine from These Grapes. New York and London: Harper and Brothers, 1934.

Conversation at Midnight. New York and London: Harper and Brothers, 1937.

Huntsman, What Quarry? New York and London: Harper and Brothers, 1939.

Make Bright the Arrows; 1940 Notebook. New York and London: Harper and Brothers, 1940.

Invocation to the Muses. New York and London: Harper and Brothers, 1941.

Collected Sonnets. New York and London: Harper and Brothers, 1941.

The Murder of Lidice. New York and London: Harper and Brothers, 1942.

Collected Lyrics. New York and London: Harper and Brothers, 1943.

Poem and Prayer for an Invading Army. New York: National Broadcasting Company, 1944.

Mine the Harvest. New York and London: Harper and Brothers, 1954.

Collected Poems. New York: Harper and Brothers, 1956.

2. Plays

Aria da Capo. First published in *Reedy's Mirror,* 18 March 1920; then in
    Chapbook (A Monthly Miscellany), no. 14 (August 1920); then by Mitch-
    ell Kennerley, 1921.
The Lamp and the Bell. New York: Frank Shay, 1921.
Two Slatterns and a King. A Moral Interlude. Cincinnati: Stewart Kidd, 1921.
The King's Henchman. New York and London: Harper and Brothers, 1927.
The Princess Marries the Page. New York and London: Harper and Brothers,
    1932.

3. Translations

"Heavenly and Earthly Love." In *All the Plays of Molnár.* New York:
    Vanguard Press, 1929.
Flowers of Evil. From the French of Charles Baudelaire, with George Dillon.
    New York and London: Harper and Brothers, 1936.

4. Letters

Burden, Jean. "With Love from Vincent," *Yankee* 22 (May 1958): 40–43,
    92–95. Incorporates letters to Millay's aunt, Susan Emery Ricker.
Carpenter, Margaret H. *Sara Teasdale.* New York: Schulte Publishing Co.,
    1960. Letters to and from Millay, pp. 166, 231–32.
Letters of Edna St. Vincent Millay. Edited by Allan Ross Macdougall. New
    York and London: Harper and Brothers, 1952.
Love, Kennett. "The Best-Known Undergraduate," *USA* 1:1 (June
    1962):74. Has a letter of late 1918 to her college friend Katherine Tilt.

5. Uncollected Writings: Poetry

Only items not included by Yost are listed.
"The Arrival." In *And Spain Sings.* Edited by M. J. Bernadete and Rolfe
    Humphries. New York: Vanguard Press, 1937, pp. 57–61. Translation
    of "Llegada" by Emilio Prados.
"The President with a Candidate's Face." *New York Herald Tribune,* 3
    November 1940, Sec. II, p. 1.
"Sonnet" [You men and women all of British birth]. *New York Times
    Magazine,* 16 February 1941, p. 2.
"Not to Be Spotted by His Blood." *New York Times Magazine,* 28 December
    1941, p. 5.
"Thanksgiving, 1942." *New York Times Magazine,* 22 November 1942, pp.
    5–6.
"For My Brother Han and My Sisters, in Holland." *New York Times Maga-
    zine,* 7 January 1945, p. 24.

"To the Leaders of the Allied Nations." *New York Times Magazine,* 21 January
   1945.
"Thanksgiving . . . 1950." *Saturday Evening Post* 223 (25 November
   1950):31.

6. Uncollected Writings: Prose
Only items not included by Yost are listed.
"My Debt to Books." *Books Abroad* 12 (Spring 1938):165.
"The Little Boy Next Door." *Talks . . . A Quarterly Digest of Addresses . . .
   Broadcast over the Columbia Network* 6 (April 1941):6. An appeal to feed
   Chinese children.
"Nothing . . . If Not Enough." *This Week Magazine,* 7 February 1943, p. 2.
   Encouragement to continue war effort.

SECONDARY SOURCES

1. Bibliographies
American Literary Manuscripts. Austin: University of Texas Press, 1960.
Kohn, John S. van E. "Some Undergraduate Printings of Edna St. Vincent
   Millay." *Publishers Weekly* 138 (30 November 1940): 2026–29.
Nierman, Judith. *Edna St. Vincent Millay: A Reference Guide.* Boston:
   G. K. Hall & Co., 1977. Annotated items in chronological order
   through 1973. Best work available on secondary material. Brief survey
   of reviewing and scholarship in introduction.
Patton, John J. "A Comprehensive Bibliography of Criticism of Edna St.
   Vincent Millay." *Serif* 5 (September 1968):10–32. Lists more than 600
   items.
**Spiller, Robert E.; Thorp, Willard; Johnson, Thomas H; and Canby,
   Henry Seidel.** *Literary History of the United States, III.* Bibliography,
   pp. 656–58. Supplement, pp. 169–70. New York: Macmillan and
   Co., 1962.
Yost, Karl. *A Bibliography of the Works of Edna St. Vincent Millay.* New York:
   Harper and Brothers, 1937. Inadequate regarding secondary material
   but indispensable for primary material through 1936.

2. Material in Books
Since Miriam Gurko's *Restless Spirit* contains an excellent bibliography, very
few items pertaining to Millay's biography are listed.

Atkins, Elizabeth. *Edna St. Vincent Millay and Her Times.* Chicago: The University of Chicago Press, 1936. An excessively adulatory work diluted by irrelevant literary history; but comments on individual works are sometimes perceptive.

Blankenship, Russell. *American Literature as an Expression of the National Mind.* New York: Henry Holt & Co., 1931. Sees Millay as a superb, essentially unphilosophical singer of the joy of living. (Not cited by Yost.)

Brenner, Rica. *Ten Modern Poets.* New York: Harcourt, Brace and Co., 1930. Indicates the poet's early bent for humor and parody.

Cargill, Oscar. *Intellectual America: Ideas on the March.* New York: Macmillan and Co., 1941. Though he thinks Millay influenced for the worse by decadence, and carelessly contributing to the moral chaos of the 1920s, he praises much and gives her credit for helping to free America from irrational taboos.

Cheney, Anne. *Millay in Greenwich Village.* University: The University of Alabama Press, 1975. An attempt at a psychological biography focusing on Millay's Village experiences and relationships with men.

Cook, Harold Lewis. "Edna St. Vincent Millay,—An Essay." In *A Bibliography of the Works of Edna St. Vincent Millay.* Edited by Karl Yost. New York: Harper and Brothers, 1937. He thinks the conservatism of woman is behind the poet's lack of analysis, her conclusiveness, her intimate presentation of warm life. He commends her accuracy, mastery of sonnet form, and breaking through restrictions placed on women writers. Millay commended Cook for understanding her poetry in "a thoughtful and lucid study."

Dash, Joan. "Edna St. Vincent Millay." In *A Life of One's Own: Three Gifted Women and the Men They Married.* New York: Harper and Row, 1973. On Millay and her husband, emphasizing her neuroticism. Most nearly psychoanalytical biography to date.

[Dell, Floyd]. "Edna St. Vincent Millay." In *The Literary Spotlight.* New York: George H. Doran Co., 1924. Perceptive regarding the multiplicity of Millay's nature, and her affectations.

Eastman, Max. "My Friendship with Edna Millay." In *Great Companions: Critical Memoirs of Some Famous Friends.* New York: Farrar, Straus and Cudahy, 1959. Valuable concerning Eastman's friendship with Millay and her husband during the 1920s and 1930s.

Gould, Jean. *The Poet and Her Book: A Biography of Edna St. Vincent Millay.* New York: Dodd, Mead and Co., 1969. Detailed, rather verbose, lightly documented.

Gray, James. *Edna St. Vincent Millay.* University of Minnesota Pamphlets on American Writers. No. 64. St. Paul: University of Minnesota Press, 1967. Millay's main theme is the search for integrity of the individual.

Gurko, Miriam. *Restless Spirit: The Life of Edna St. Vincent Millay.* New York: Thomas Y. Crowell Co., 1962. Good biography, addressed especially to readers of high-school age. Emphasizes Millay's volatility and elusiveness as a subject; contains excellent bibliography relating to the poet's life.

Kreymborg, Alfred. *Our Singing Strength.* New York: Coward-McCann, Inc., 1929. Comments on individual poems. (Not cited by Yost.)

Loggins, Vernon. *I Hear America . . . Literature in the United States Since 1900.* New York: Thomas Y. Crowell Co., 1937. Rapid but discriminating review. Millay still a minor poet.

Madeleva, Sister M. "Where Are You Going, My Pretty Maid?" In *Chaucer's Nuns and Other Essays.* New York: D. Appleton and Co., 1925. Shrewd, level-headed assessment of Millay's poetic successes, weaknesses, and potentialities up to 1925.

Shafter, Toby. *Edna St. Vincent Millay, America's Best-Loved Poet.* New York: Julian Messner, 1957. Inaccurate and inadequate work for juvenile readers.

Sheehan, Vincent. *The Indigo Bunting: A Memoir of Edna St. Vincent Millay.* New York: Harper and Brothers, 1951. Throws light on Millay's way of life and interests in the 1940s, especially her long-continued interest in birds.

Stanbrough, Jane. "Edna St. Vincent Millay and the Language of Vulnerability." In *Shakespeare's Sisters: Feminist Essays on Women Poets.* Edited, with an Introduction by Sandra M. Gilbert and Susan Gubar. Bloomington and London: Indiana University Press, 1978. Stresses Millay's feelings for women's victimization and her own vulnerability and anguish.

Untermeyer, Louis. *American Poetry since 1900.* New York: Harcourt, Brace and Co., 1923. Praises Millay's intensity, capacity for ecstasy, and felicity of language; disparages facile cynicism of *A Few Figs.*

Van Doren, Carl. "Youth and Wings: Edna St. Vincent Millay." In *Many Minds.* New York: Alfred A. Knopf, 1924. Appreciative analysis.

Wilson, Edmund. "Epilogue, 1952: Edna St. Vincent Millay." In *The Shores of Light: A Literary Chronicle of the Twenties and Thirties.* New York: Farrar, Straus and Young, Inc., 1952. A significant account of personal acquaintance during Greenwich Village period and of some later encounters, especially near the end of Millay's life.

3. Articles, Essays, and Reviews

Benét, William Rose. "Round About Parnassus." *Saturday Review of Literature* 11 (10 November 1934):279. On *Wine From These Grapes*. Finds evidence of development.

Breuer, Elizabeth. "Edna St. Vincent Millay." *Pictorial Review* 33 (November 1931):2. An excellent account of Steepletop life, Millay's habits and attitudes, and the philosophy of her marriage.

Brittin, Norman A. "Edna St. Vincent Millay's 'Nancy Boyd' Stories." *Ball State University Forum* 10 (Spring 1969):31–36. Analyzes stories in *Ainslee's* and relates them to Millay's life and personality.

Colum, Padraic. "Miss Millay's Poems." *Freeman* 4 (2 November 1921):189–90. Judicious assigning of praise and blame which distinguishes between childlike and mature.

Curley, Francis X. "Edna St. Vincent Millay." *America* 84 (11 November 1950):166–68. Praise of sharp observation of nature, craftsmanship, and sincerity in *Fatal Interview* (with detailed analysis of Sonnet XI).

Dabbs, James McBride. "Edna St. Vincent Millay: Not Resigned." *South Atlantic Quarterly* 37 (January 1938):54–66. An interesting analysis that takes Millay to task for lacking resignation but eventually finds her forced to write as she has done because of her situation in respect to religious tradition.

Davison, Edward. "Edna St. Vincent Millay." *English Journal* 16 (1927):671–82. Though placing her high among her American contemporaries, he confines the poet to a relatively minor position. Objects to the sensational, seamy, and flippant in her work, praises fine lyrics but thinks Millay has no consistent scheme of values by which to measure the world, and thus cannot achieve greatness.

DuBois, A. E. "Edna St. Vincent Millay." *Sewanee Review* 43 (1935):80–104. A penetrating psychological analysis showing Millay as a combination of precocious and spoiled child, pure poet, woman, and mystic. (Not cited by Yost.)

Gregory, Horace. "Edna St. Vincent Millay, Poet and Legend." *New York Herald Tribune Books,* 11 November 1934, p. 3. On *Wine from These Grapes*.

Hackett, Francis. "Edna St. Vincent Millay." *New Republic* 135 (24 December 1956):21–22. Tribute to Millay's greatness, focused on *Collected Poems.* Her poetry expresses desire for emancipation, scorn of evasion, a large sense of America, reverence for life and indignation at its abuse. She explores the tragic sense of our time.

Hay, Sara Henderson. "The Unpersuadable V." *Saturday Review* 37 (5 June 1954):20. Good summary of Millay's most important qualities.

Hill, Frank Ernest. "Edna St. Vincent Millay." *Measure,* no. 1 (March 1921), pp. 25–26. On *A Few Figs from Thistles.* Points out the dominance of the dramatic in Millay's work. (Not cited by Yost.)

Klemans, Patricia A. "'Being Born a Woman': A New Look at Edna St. Vincent Millay." *Colby Library Quarterly* 15 (March 1979):7–18. Praises Millay for her timeless message of feminine individuality, and explains Millay's methods of attaining universality in *Fatal Interview.*

McInnis, Edgar. "The New Writers—Edna St. Vincent Millay." *Canadian Forum* 11 (August 1931):424–25. Finds Millay's work uneven, best when she combines simplicity and sincerity in her less experimental poetry.

Monroe, Harriet. "Advance or Retreat?" *Poetry* 38 (July 1931):216–21. On *Fatal Interview.*

———. "Edna St. Vincent Millay." *Poetry* 24 (August 1924):260–66. Emphasizes Millay's truthfulness and sincerity, with special praise for her sonnets.

O'F., S. "Literature and Life. Edna St. Vincent Millay." *Irish Statesman* 12 (1929):213–14. Finds *The Buck in the Snow* mature, like Yeats of middle period; praises her technical ability, her use of homely image and simple word. (Not cited by Yost.)

Parks, Edd Winfield. "Edna St. Vincent Millay." *Sewanee Review* 38 (January 1930):42–49. Thinks Millay, a poet of beautiful but narrow range, emotional and unphilosophical, has been moved by the discipline of writing *The King's Henchman* and by the Sacco-Vanzetti affair to more experimental techniques, more objective poetry, and perhaps to becoming a greater, more philosophical poet.

Preston, John H. "Edna St. Vincent Millay." *Virginia Quarterly Review* 3 (1927):342–55. Strong approval of Millay's sensuous paganism, nearness to elemental things, and especially *The King's Henchman* and the sonnets.

Ransom, John Crowe. "The Poet as Woman." *Southern Review* 2 (Spring 1937):783–806. Reprinted in *The World's Body.* New York and London: Charles Scribner's Sons, 1938. Exposes some of Atkins's inadequacies; thinks Millay lacking in intellectual interest, too unlike Donne, but typically a woman artist. Unintentionally patronizing.

Scott, Winfield Townley. "Millay Collected." *Poetry* 63 (March 1944:334–42. Millay's work suffers from repetitiousness, self-pity, sentimentality, overdone emotion, and loss of humor; but she always had integrity, and much of her poetry shows sharp observation, power and passion.

Taggard, Genevieve. "A Woman's Anatomy of Love." *New York Herald Tribune Books,* 19 April 1931, p. 3. On *Fatal Interview.* Praises Millay as a traditional writer, accounts for her special success in sonnets.

Tate, Allen. "Miss Millay's Sonnets." *New Republic* 66 (6 May 1931):335–36. (A systematically modified version of this is in *Reactionary Essays on Poetry and Ideas.* New York: Charles Scribner's Sons, 1936). Finds Millay a distinguished poet of the second rank (a sensibility, not an intellect) who created a personal idiom from traditional symbols and nineteeth-century vocabulary. *Fatal Interview* a very skillfull sustained performance in the Shakespearean form.

Watkins, Mary F. "Operatic Events of the Past Month." *Musical Observer* 26 (April 1927):12, 38–39. The most informative early assessment of *The King's Henchman.* (Not cited by Yost.)

4. Unpublished Dissertations

King, Grace Hamilton. *The Development of the Social Consciousness of Edna St. Vincent Millay as Manifested in Her Poetry.* Dissertation, New York University, 1943. Millay's social consciousness was initiated through reading, furthered by Greenwich Village experiences, the Sacco-Vanzetti case, and the rise of fascism and communism. Important because it contains Millay's views expressed in an interview of 1941.

Minot, Walter S. *Edna St. Vincent Millay: A Critical Revaluation.* Dissertation, University of Nebraska, 1972. Ann Arbor, Mich.: University Microfilms, Inc., no. 79–2911. Finds Millay a worthy minor poet unjustly neglected and demonstrates her poetic experimentation and development. Some analyses of poems are helpful.

Patton, John Joseph. *Edna St. Vincent Millay as a Verse Dramatist.* Dissertation, University of Colorado, 1962. Ann Arbor, Mich.: University Microfilms, Inc., No. 63–2006. A thorough study which gives Millay much credit for perpetuating verse drama with six effective plays.

Petitt, Jean Morris. *Edna St. Vincent Millay: A Critical Study of Her Poetry in Its Social and Literary Milieu.* Dissertation, Vanderbilt University, 1955. Ann Arbor, Mich.: University Microfilms, Inc., Doctoral Dissertation Series, No. 15,799. Although it contains many annoying slips and the author is insensitive to much of Millay's best work, it provides some understanding of the literary milieu. Asserts that the poet had strong religious faith and that her poetry, in its intense emotionality, is that of the last American Romantic.

Index

DATE DUE

GAYLORD			PRINTED IN U.S.A.